FATHERING STRONG

A 90-Day Devotional Journey

Bruce Stapleton

MOVEMENTUM
PRESS

FATHERING STRONG
A 90-Day Devotional Journey

Published by Movementum Press
WWW.MOVEMENTUM.COM

This book is a work of non-fiction. Unless otherwise noted, the author and the publisher make no explicit guarantees as to the accuracy of the information in this book.

This book is a part of the Fathering Strong Fatherhood Series of publications and may be ordered by going to www.fatheringstrongbook.com.
Other resources that accompany this book include:
Fathering Strong – God's Blueprint for Leading Your Family
Fatherhood Awakening and 30-day Devotional and Journal

Because of the dynamic nature of the Internet, any web addresses or links contained in this book may have changed since publication and may no longer be valid.

Scripture quotations are taken from the Holy Bible, NEW INTERNATIONAL VERSION, NIV Copyright© 1973, 1978, 1984, 2011 by Biblica, Inc. Used by permission. All rights reserved worldwide.

Scripture quotations are from the ESV® Bible (The Holy Bible, English Standard Version®), copyright© 2001 by Crossway Bibles, a publishing ministry of Good News Publishers. Used by permission. All rights reserved.

ISBN: 979-8-9985544-7-6

Table of Contents

Introduction: Your 90-Day Journey to Fathering Strong

The weight of fatherhood hit me the moment I held my newborn daughter for the first time. Her tiny fingers wrapped around mine, and in that instant, I felt an overwhelming mix of joy, wonder, and — if I'm honest — sheer terror. I made a silent promise to be the best father I could be, to guide her, protect her, and help her grow into a strong, confident woman. But as any father knows, good intentions alone aren't enough. The journey of fatherhood requires something deeper, something more enduring than momentary enthusiasm or fleeting determination.

Maybe you're feeling that same mix of emotions right now. Perhaps you're a new dad, still learning how to change diapers and decode different cries. Or maybe you've been at this for years, navigating the complex waters of raising teenagers or watching your adult children build their own lives. Wherever you are in your fatherhood journey, you've likely discovered this truth: being a father is one of life's greatest privileges and most demanding challenges.

This 90-day devotional is designed to help you build an unshakeable foundation for your fatherhood — not through quick fixes or simple formulas, but through the cultivation of four essential virtues that have sustained faithful fathers throughout history: **courage, fortitude, faith, and love**.

Why These Four Virtues?

Think of these virtues as the four legs of a table. When one is weak, everything on top becomes unstable. But when all four are strong and balanced, they can support the weight of whatever life places upon them. The same is true for fatherhood.

Courage is where your journey begins. It's the virtue that gets you started, that helps you take that first step into intentional fatherhood even when you don't feel ready. Courage means facing your fears head-on — whether that's admitting you don't have all the answers, having difficult conversations with your children, or standing firm on unpopular decisions. As Joshua 1:9 reminds us, "Have I not commanded you? Be strong and courageous. Do not be afraid; do not be discouraged, for the LORD your God will be with you wherever you go."

I remember the courage it took to admit to my kids that I'd made a mistake in handling a family situation. My pride wanted to defend my actions, but courage meant saying, "I was wrong, and I'm sorry." That moment of vulnerability actually strengthened our relationship more than a thousand "perfect" parenting moments ever could. Courage isn't about being fearless — it's about acting despite your fears, driven by love for your children and commitment to your calling.

Fortitude is what keeps you going when courage alone isn't enough. If courage gets you started, fortitude sustains you through the long haul. It's the enduring strength that carries you through sleepless nights with a newborn, challenging teenage years, financial pressures, and every trial in between. Like the mighty oak that bends but doesn't break during fierce storms, fathers with fortitude grow stronger through adversity.

Fortitude is what enabled my friend David to keep showing up for his son during a two-year battle with addiction. It's what gave another father the strength to work three jobs while learning English at night, all to ensure his daughters could have the education he never received. As James 1:2-4 teaches us, "Consider it pure joy, my brothers and sisters, whenever you face trials of many kinds, because you know that the testing of your faith produces perseverance. Let perseverance finish its work so that you may be mature and complete, not lacking anything."

Faith provides the foundation that holds everything together. It's the deep-rooted belief in something greater than ourselves — a source of strength that carries us through our toughest days. Faith isn't just about religious practice (though that may be part of your journey); it's about trusting in God's wisdom when your own runs out, believing in His promises when circumstances suggest

2

otherwise, and finding meaning in the sacred calling of fatherhood.

Faith is what sustained me when my daughter was struggling with self-doubt about her future. It's what gave another father peace when his son was diagnosed with autism, helping him see that every small victory was a blessing to be celebrated. Whether through prayer, meditation, service to others, or simply a deep-seated belief in something greater than ourselves, faith provides the foundation upon which we build our legacy as fathers. As Proverbs 3:5-6 instructs us, "Trust in the LORD with all your heart and lean not on your own understanding; in all your ways submit to him, and he will make your paths straight."

Love is the virtue that fuels everything else. While courage, fortitude, and faith are crucial, there's one virtue that gives them all meaning and purpose: love. As 1 Corinthians 16:14 reminds us, "Do everything in love." Without love, courage becomes recklessness, fortitude becomes stubbornness, and faith becomes empty religion. But with love, everything changes. Love transforms duty into delight, obligation into opportunity, and sacrifice into joy.

Love is what gets you up at 3 AM with a sick child. It's what keeps you patient during the hundredth explanation of homework. It's what drives you to your knees in prayer when your teenager is making choices that break your heart. Love isn't just a feeling—it's a choice, a commitment, an action. It's showing up day after day, even when you're tired, even when you're discouraged, even when you don't see immediate results.

How This Devotional Works

Over the next 90 days, you'll spend time developing each of these four virtues:

- **Days 1-22: Courage** - The Foundation of Faithful Fatherhood

- **Days 23-44: Fortitude** - Enduring Strength for the Long Journey

3

- **Days 45-66: Faith** - The Foundation That Holds Everything Together

- **Days 67-90: Love** - The Virtue That Fuels Everything Else

Each day includes:

- A **Word of the Day** to focus your thoughts

- A **Scripture Reading** to ground you in God's truth

- A **Reflection** that combines biblical wisdom with real-world application

- Practical insights for your daily walk as a father

Starting on Day 35, your devotional experience will be enhanced with two additional powerful sections. **Fathering Strong Insights** will provide deeper, more targeted wisdom specifically designed to challenge and support your growth as a father. The **Today's Challenge** section will offer a practical, actionable step you can take immediately to apply the day's lessons, helping you transform insight into meaningful action. These new sections are crafted to propel you further on your journey of intentional, Christ-centered fatherhood.

This isn't just another book to read—it's a journey to walk. Some days will challenge you. Some will comfort you. Some will convict you. All of them are designed to help you grow into the father God has called you to be.

A Word of Encouragement

Let me be honest with you: you're going to have days when you feel like you're failing. Days when you lose your temper, when you're too tired to be present, when you make the wrong call. I've been there. Every father has. But here's the beautiful truth of the Gospel: God's mercies are new every morning (Lamentations 3:22-23). Every single day is an opportunity to start fresh, to make different choices, to move in a new direction.

You don't have to be a perfect father. You just need to be a faithful one—a man who keeps showing up, keeps growing, keeps trying, and keeps trusting God to fill in the gaps where you fall short.

Your children don't need a superhero. They need a present, engaged father who loves them unconditionally, who models what it means to follow God imperfectly but persistently, and who creates a home where grace abounds and love never fails.

Before You Begin

As you start this 90-day journey, I encourage you to:

1. **Find a consistent time and place** for your daily reading. Whether it's early morning before the house wakes up or late evening after the kids are in bed, consistency will help you build this into your rhythm.

2. **Keep a journal** nearby. Write down your thoughts, prayers, and commitments. Document your journey so you can look back and see how God has worked in your life.

3. **Find an accountability partner**—another father who can walk this journey with you, someone you can be honest with about your struggles and victories.

4. **Be patient with yourself**. Growth takes time. Some virtues will come more naturally than others. That's okay. The goal isn't perfection—it's progress.

5. **Pray before you read**. Ask God to speak to you through His Word and through these reflections. Ask Him to show you specific ways to apply what you're learning.

Your Legacy Starts Today

The decisions you make today as a father will echo through generations. The character you develop, the love you show, the faith you model—all of it creates a legacy that will outlive you. Your children are watching, learning, and being shaped by your example every single day.

But you're not alone in this journey. The same God who commanded Joshua to be strong and courageous is the same God who walks with you today. The same God who gave Paul strength for every challenge is the same God who will strengthen you. The same God who is described as the perfect Father in heaven is the same God who will teach you how to father your children on earth.

So let's begin this journey together. Over the next 90 days, we'll explore what it means to father with courage, to endure with fortitude, to lead with faith, and to love without limits. We'll discover that Fathering Strong isn't about being the biggest, the toughest, or the most successful — it's about being faithful, present, and anchored in the unchanging character of God.

Your children are worth this investment. Your family is worth this commitment. And you — yes, you — are capable of becoming the father God designed you to be.

Let's get started.

"Finally, be strong in the Lord and in his mighty power. Put on the full armor of God, so that you can take your stand against the devil's schemes." — Ephesians 6:10-11

DAYS 1-22: COURAGE - The Foundation of Faithful Fatherhood

Notes

Day 1: The Call to Courageous Fatherhood

Word of the Day: INITIATE

Scripture Reading: Joshua 1:9 (NIV)
"Have I not commanded you? Be strong and courageous. Do not be afraid; do not be discouraged, for the LORD your God will be with you wherever you go."

Reflection:

The journey of fatherhood begins with a single, courageous step—the decision to lead your family with intentionality and purpose. God's command to Joshua wasn't a suggestion or a gentle encouragement; it was a divine mandate backed by an unshakeable promise. The same God who commanded Joshua to be strong and courageous is the same God who calls you today to rise up as the spiritual leader of your home. This isn't about perfection; it's about direction. It's about making the conscious choice to stop drifting through fatherhood and start driving toward a God-honoring legacy.

Courage in fatherhood means taking the initiative even when you don't feel ready, even when you're uncertain about the outcome, even when past failures whisper lies about your inadequacy. Every great father in Scripture—Abraham, Moses, David—faced moments of profound uncertainty, yet they moved forward in obedience to God's call. Your family doesn't need a perfect father; they need a present one. They need a man who will stand in the gap, who will fight for their hearts, who will model what it means to trust God even when the path ahead is unclear. Today marks the beginning of your intentional journey toward becoming the father God designed you to be.

Day 2: Facing Your Fears

Word of the Day: CONFRONT

Scripture Reading: 2 Timothy 1:7 (ESV)
"For God gave us a spirit not of fear but of power and love and self-control."

Reflection:

Every father carries fears — fear of failure, fear of inadequacy, fear of repeating the mistakes of previous generations, fear of not providing enough, fear of losing influence with your children as they grow. These fears are real, but they are not from God. The spirit of fear is a counterfeit that seeks to paralyze you, to keep you from stepping into the fullness of your calling as a father. God has given you something far more powerful: a spirit of power, love, and self-control. This divine gift equips you to face every challenge, every uncertainty, every moment of doubt with confidence rooted not in your own strength but in His.

Courageous fatherhood requires you to name your fears, bring them into the light, and surrender them to God. What specific anxieties keep you awake at night? What worries prevent you from being fully present with your children? The enemy wants you to believe that acknowledging fear is weakness, but the opposite is true. It takes tremendous courage to be honest about your struggles, to admit that you don't have all the answers, to confess that you need God's help every single day. When you confront your fears head-on, you rob them of their power. You demonstrate to your children that real strength isn't the absence of fear — it's the decision to move forward despite it. Today, identify one fear that has been holding you back and take one concrete step toward facing it with God's help.

Day 3: Setting Boundaries with Love

Word of the Day: PROTECT

Scripture Reading: Proverbs 4:23 (NIV)
"Above all else, guard your heart, for everything you do flows from it."

Reflection:

One of the most courageous acts of fatherhood is establishing and maintaining healthy boundaries for your family. In a culture that celebrates unlimited access, constant connectivity, and the erosion of traditional values, setting boundaries can feel countercultural and uncomfortable. Yet boundaries are not restrictions designed to limit joy; they are protective barriers that create space for your family to flourish. When you set boundaries around screen time, you're protecting your children's minds and preserving precious family connection. When you establish boundaries around the influences you allow into your home, you're guarding the spiritual atmosphere of your household. When you create boundaries around your own time and commitments, you're demonstrating that your family is your priority.

Setting boundaries requires courage because it often means saying no—to opportunities, to social pressure, to your children's temporary displeasure, even your own desires. It means being willing to be the "bad guy" in the moment for the sake of long-term good. It means standing firm when everyone else seems to be compromising. But here's the truth: your children may not thank you now for the boundaries you set, but they will thank you later when they realize those boundaries kept them safe, shaped their character, and taught them the value of self-discipline. Boundaries communicate love. They say, "You matter too much to me to let you wander into danger." They say, "Our family has a higher calling than simply fitting in with the world around us." Today, evaluate one area where your family needs clearer boundaries, and have the courage to establish them with love and consistency.

Day 4: The Courage to Admit Mistakes

Word of the Day: HUMBLE

Scripture Reading: James 5:16 (NIV)
"Therefore confess your sins to each other and pray for each other so that you may be healed. The prayer of a righteous person is powerful and effective."

Reflection:

Perhaps no act of courage is more powerful in fatherhood than the willingness to admit when you're wrong. Pride whispers that acknowledging mistakes will diminish your authority, that showing vulnerability will weaken your position as leader of your home. But the opposite is true. When you have the humility to say "I was wrong" or "I'm sorry" to your children, you don't lose respect—you gain it. You demonstrate that integrity matters more than image, that relationships matter more than reputation, that growth matters more than always being right. Your children don't need a father who pretends to be perfect; they need a father who models what it looks like to fail, repent, and get back up again.

Admitting mistakes creates a culture of grace in your home. When your children see you taking responsibility for your actions, they learn that mistakes are not catastrophic failures but opportunities for growth. They learn that character is built not in perfection but in how we respond when we fall short. They learn that real strength includes the ability to be vulnerable, to acknowledge weakness, to seek forgiveness. This kind of humility breaks generational cycles of pride and defensiveness. It opens doors for authentic conversation and deep connection. It teaches your children that they can come to you with their own failures without fear of harsh judgment. Today, if there's an unresolved conflict with your child, if there's a moment where you responded in anger or impatience, have the courage to go to them, look them in the eye, and say, "I was wrong. Will you forgive me?" This simple act of humility will do more to build your relationship than a thousand lectures ever could.

Day 5: Standing Against Cultural Currents

Word of the Day: COUNTERCULTURAL

Scripture Reading: Romans 12:2 (ESV)
"Do not be conformed to this world, but be transformed by the renewal of your mind, that by testing you may discern what is the will of God, what is good and acceptable and perfect."

Reflection:

To father with courage today means swimming against cultural currents that seek to redefine masculinity, family, and truth. The pressure to conform is immense — to lower standards, compromise convictions, prioritize temporary happiness over eternal well-being. But God calls you to be transformed, not conformed. To lead your family by His blueprint, not the world's. This requires courage because you'll often stand alone, face criticism, and your children may temporarily resent the standards you uphold.

Standing against culture doesn't mean being angry or isolated. It means being anchored in truth while engaging with grace. Teaching your children to think critically, evaluate everything through Scripture, and recognize that popularity and truth aren't synonymous. Your home should be a lighthouse — a place of stability and truth amid shifting values.

This requires daily intentionality. Monitor what influences enter through media, friendships, and activities. Have courageous conversations about difficult topics before culture shapes your children's thinking. Be willing to make unpopular decisions because you're more concerned with God's approval than man's applause. Today, identify one area where cultural pressure is strongest in your family's life, and make a courageous decision to align with God's truth rather than cultural trends

Day 6: The Courage to Be Present

Word of the Day: ATTENTIVE

Scripture Reading: Deuteronomy 6:6-7 (NIV)
"These commandments that I give you today are to be on your hearts. Impress them on your children. Talk about them when you sit at home and when you walk along the road, when you lie down and when you get up."

Reflection:

In an age of constant distraction, one of the most courageous choices you can make as a father is to be fully present with your family. Presence is more than physical proximity; it's emotional availability, mental focus, and spiritual attentiveness. It's putting down your phone when your child wants to talk, turning off the game to hear about their day, being mentally engaged during dinner instead of rehearsing tomorrow's meeting.

The courage to be present requires fighting against the tyranny of the urgent and the addiction to productivity. Your most important work isn't happening at the office—it's happening at the dinner table, in the car on the way to practice, during bedtime prayers, in spontaneous conversations when you're simply available. Moses instructed the Israelites to teach their children throughout daily life—sitting at home, walking along the road, lying down, getting up. This teaching doesn't happen in scheduled sessions; it happens in the margins, in mundane moments, when you're present enough to recognize and seize the opportunities God provides.

Your children spell love T-I-M-E. They need your presence more than your presents, your attention more than your achievements, your engagement more than your income. Today, commit to being fully present for at least one hour with your family—no phone, no distractions, just focused attention on the people who matter most.

Day 7: Modeling Integrity in the Small Things

Word of the Day: CONSISTENT

Scripture Reading: Luke 16:10 (NIV)
"Whoever can be trusted with very little can also be trusted with much, and whoever is dishonest with very little will also be dishonest with much."

Reflection:

Your children are watching you in the small moments—how you respond when the cashier gives you too much change, what you say about your boss, whether you follow through on small promises, how you treat the server at the restaurant. These seemingly insignificant moments are actually the most significant because they reveal your true character. Integrity isn't what you do on Sunday morning when everyone is watching; it's what you do on Tuesday afternoon when no one is.

Courageous fatherhood means recognizing that you're always teaching, always modeling, always shaping your children's understanding of character. You can't lecture your children into integrity; you can only live it in front of them consistently, day after day, choice after choice. When you admit you were wrong about something small, you teach them humility. When you return the extra change, you teach them honesty. When you keep your promise to play catch even though you're tired, you teach them reliability. When you speak respectfully about others, you teach them honor.

These small acts of integrity compound over time, creating a legacy of trustworthiness that will shape your children's character for generations. The question isn't whether you'll be perfect—you won't. The question is whether you'll be consistent in pursuing integrity even in the small things. Today, pay attention to the small choices you make, and let each one be an opportunity to model the character you want to see in your children.

Day 8: The Courage to Discipline with Love

Word of the Day: CORRECT

Scripture Reading: Proverbs 3:11-12 (ESV)
"My son, do not despise the LORD's discipline or be weary of his reproof, for the LORD reproves him whom he loves, as a father the son in whom he delights."

Reflection:

One of the most challenging aspects of courageous fatherhood is the responsibility to discipline your children. In a culture that often confuses discipline with abuse and boundaries with lack of love, many fathers have abdicated this crucial role. But Scripture is clear: discipline is an expression of love, not a contradiction of it. When you correct your children, you're shaping their character, teaching them that actions have consequences, and ultimately pointing them toward the loving discipline of their Heavenly Father.

Effective discipline requires courage because it's often uncomfortable and emotionally taxing. It's easier to let things slide, to avoid conflict, to be the "fun parent" who never says no. But this permissiveness isn't love—it's neglect. Biblical discipline is always purposeful, proportionate, and rooted in relationship. It's not about venting anger or asserting power; it's about teaching, training, and guiding your children toward wisdom and maturity. It requires consistency, follow-through, and remaining calm even when frustrated. You must always communicate that your love is unconditional even when their behavior is unacceptable.

The goal of discipline isn't compliance; it's character. It's not about controlling your children; it's about equipping them to control themselves. Today, if there's an area where you've been avoiding necessary discipline, have the courage to address it with love, clarity, and consistency.

Day 9: Facing Financial Fears with Faith

Word of the Day: STEWARD

Scripture Reading: Matthew 6:31-33 (NIV)
"So do not worry, saying, 'What shall we eat?' or 'What shall we drink?' or 'What shall we wear?' For the pagans run after all these things, and your heavenly Father knows that you need them. But seek first his kingdom and his righteousness, and all these things will be given to you as well."

Reflection:

Financial pressure is one of the greatest sources of fear for fathers. The weight of provision, anxiety about the future, comparison with others, the fear of not giving your children enough — these concerns can be overwhelming. But God calls you to courage through faith in His provision and wisdom in your stewardship. You are not the ultimate provider; God is. Your role is to be a faithful steward, to work diligently, manage wisely, and trust Him for the outcome.

Courageous financial leadership means making decisions based on values rather than fear, on long-term wisdom rather than short-term pressure. It means honest conversations with your wife about money, creating and sticking to a budget, saying no to lifestyle inflation, teaching your children the difference between wants and needs, and modeling contentment. It means making sacrifices now for financial freedom later, trusting that God's provision is sufficient even when it doesn't match your expectations or your neighbor's lifestyle.

Financial courage also means being generous — giving to your church, supporting those in need, and teaching your children that money is a tool for kingdom purposes. Today, take one practical step: create or review your budget, have an honest money conversation with your spouse, or identify one area to increase giving or decrease spending.

Day 10: The Courage to Pray Out Loud

Word of the Day: INTERCEDE

Scripture Reading: 1 Thessalonians 5:16-18 (ESV)
"Rejoice always, pray without ceasing, give thanks in all circumstances; for this is the will of God in Christ Jesus for you."

Reflection:

For many men, praying out loud—especially in front of their families—requires significant courage. There's vulnerability in speaking to God in the presence of others, in letting your family hear your doubts, your requests, your gratitude, your dependence on God. Yet this act of spiritual leadership is one of the most powerful ways you can influence your family. When your children hear you pray, they learn what matters to you. They hear you bringing real concerns to God. They witness your dependence on Him. They see that prayer isn't just a religious ritual but a genuine conversation with a loving Father. They learn that it's okay to be honest with God, to ask for help, to express gratitude, to intercede for others.

Praying out loud as a father doesn't require eloquence or theological precision. It requires authenticity and consistency. Pray at meals. Pray at bedtime. Pray when challenges arise. Pray when blessings come. Pray for your children by name, speaking God's promises over their lives. Pray for your wife, honoring her in the presence of your children. Pray for wisdom in decisions. Pray for protection over your home. Pray for opportunities to serve others. Your prayers don't need to be long or impressive; they need to be real. When you pray regularly in front of your family, you're establishing prayer as a normal, essential part of life. You're teaching your children that God is accessible, that He cares about the details of their lives, that no concern is too small or too large to bring before Him. Today, if you haven't been praying out loud with your family, start. Gather them together, even if just for a minute, and simply talk to God in their presence. Let them hear your heart for them and your dependence on Him.

Day 11: Breaking Generational Patterns

Word of the Day: TRANSFORM

Scripture Reading: Ezekiel 18:19-20 (NIV)
"Yet you ask, 'Why does the son not share the guilt of his father?' Since the son has done what is just and right and has been careful to keep all my decrees, he will surely live. The one who sins is the one who will die. The child will not share the guilt of the parent, nor will the parent share the guilt of the child."

Reflection:

One of the most courageous acts of fatherhood is the decision to break negative generational patterns. Perhaps you grew up with an absent father, an angry father, an addicted father, or an emotionally distant father. Perhaps your childhood was marked by dysfunction, abuse, or neglect. The enemy wants you to believe that you're destined to repeat these patterns. But God's Word declares something different: you have the power, through Christ, to break the cycle. You are not bound by your past. You can be the father you needed but didn't have.

Breaking generational patterns requires courage because it means doing what's unfamiliar, what you didn't see modeled, what feels uncomfortable because it's new. It means seeking help — through counseling, mentorship, or accountability — to address wounds you may not even fully recognize. It means being intentional about learning what healthy fatherhood looks like.

But here's the beautiful truth: when you break a negative generational pattern, you don't just change your children's lives — you change your grandchildren's lives and your great-grandchildren's lives. You become a generational pivot point, the father who said, "It stops with me." Today, identify one negative pattern from your past that you're determined not to repeat, and take one concrete step toward establishing a new, healthier pattern in your family.

Day 12: The Courage to Show Affection

Word of the Day: TENDER

Scripture Reading: 1 Thessalonians 2:7-8 (NIV)
"Instead, we were like young children among you. Just as a nursing mother cares for her children, so we cared for you. Because we loved you so much, we were delighted to share with you not only the gospel of God but our lives as well."

Reflection:

Many men struggle with showing physical and verbal affection to their children, especially as they grow older. Perhaps you didn't receive affection from your own father. Perhaps you've absorbed cultural messages that equate masculinity with emotional distance. Perhaps you fear that showing tenderness will somehow weaken your authority or make your children "soft." But Scripture paints a different picture of godly masculinity—one that includes tenderness, affection, and emotional availability. Paul compared his care for the Thessalonians to that of a nursing mother. Jesus welcomed children, blessed them, and held them. God Himself is described as a Father who runs to embrace His returning prodigal son.

Your children desperately need your affection. They need to hear you say "I love you" regularly. They need hugs, high-fives, pats on the back, and physical touch that communicates safety and belonging. They need to hear you speak words of affirmation, encouragement, and blessing. This kind of affection doesn't undermine your authority; it strengthens it. It creates emotional security that allows your children to take healthy risks, develop confidence, and form secure attachments. Children who receive regular affection from their fathers are less likely to seek validation in unhealthy relationships and more likely to develop healthy self-esteem. Today, make it a point to show physical affection to each of your children and to speak words of love. If this feels uncomfortable, do it anyway.

Day 13: Courage in Career Decisions

Word of the Day: PRIORITIZE

Scripture Reading: Mark 8:36 (ESV)
"For what does it profit a man to gain the whole world and forfeit his soul?"

Reflection:

Your career is important, but it's not ultimate. God has called you to provide for your family and work with excellence, but He has not called you to sacrifice your family on the altar of career success. One of the most courageous decisions you'll make as a father is how to navigate the tension between professional ambition and family priorities. The world will constantly pressure you to climb higher, earn more, and work longer. But at the end of your life, no one will wish they had spent more time at the office. Your children won't remember the promotions you earned; they'll remember whether you were present for their games, their struggles, and their celebrations.

Courageous career decisions might mean turning down a promotion that requires excessive travel. It might mean setting boundaries around work hours, even when colleagues are working around the clock. It might mean choosing a less prestigious position that allows you to be more present with your family. It might mean having honest conversations with your employer about your priorities and negotiating arrangements that honor both your professional responsibilities and your family commitments. This doesn't mean being lazy in your work; it means being intentional about ensuring that your career serves your family rather than your family serving your career.

Today, evaluate your current work-life balance honestly. Are there changes you need to make? Conversations you need to have? Boundaries you need to establish? Have the courage to prioritize your family, trusting that God will honor your faithfulness.

Day 14: The Courage to Seek Help

Word of the Day: VULNERABLE

Scripture Reading: Proverbs 11:14 (NIV)
"For lack of guidance a nation falls, but victory is won through many advisers."

Reflection:

Pride tells you that real men figure things out on their own, that asking for help is weakness, that admitting struggle means you're failing. But wisdom tells you something different: seeking help is a sign of strength, not weakness. It takes courage to admit you don't have all the answers, to acknowledge you're in over your head, to reach out for guidance or professional help. Whether you're struggling with anger, addiction, depression, marriage problems, or parenting challenges, trying to handle it alone isn't noble—it's foolish. God designed you to live in community, to benefit from the wisdom and experience of others.

Seeking help might mean finding a mentor—an older, wiser father who can guide you through challenges he's already navigated. It might mean joining a men's group where you can be honest about your struggles. It might mean seeking professional counseling to address past wounds or mental health concerns. It might mean having a vulnerable conversation with your pastor, a trusted friend, or your wife. The enemy wants to isolate you, to convince you that you're the only one facing these challenges, that admitting struggle will result in judgment. But the truth is that every father struggles. Every man faces battles. The difference between those who overcome and those who remain stuck is often simply the willingness to reach out for help. Today, if you're facing a challenge that feels overwhelming, have the courage to reach out—make the call, send the text, schedule the appointment. Seeking help isn't giving up; it's gearing up for victory.

Day 15: Courage to Have Difficult Conversations

Word of the Day: HONEST

Scripture Reading: Ephesians 4:15 (ESV)
"Rather, speaking the truth in love, we are to grow up in every way into him who is the head, into Christ."

Reflection:

Some of the most important conversations you'll have with your children are also the most difficult — conversations about sex, peer pressure, faith and doubt, failure and disappointment, cultural issues that challenge biblical values, and struggles both theirs and yours. Many fathers avoid these conversations because they're uncomfortable, fear saying the wrong thing, don't know how to start, or hope someone else will handle it. But your children need to hear truth from you, in the context of relationship, spoken with love and grace. If you don't have these conversations, the culture will.

Courageous communication means initiating conversations rather than waiting for your children to come to you. It means creating an environment where no topic is off-limits, where questions are welcomed, where honesty is valued more than having all the right answers. It means being willing to share your own struggles, to admit when you don't know something, to say "That's a great question — let me think about that and get back to you." It means speaking truth clearly while also listening deeply, seeking to understand your children's perspectives and concerns. These conversations won't always go smoothly. Your children might push back, disagree, or shut down. But the courage to keep trying will pay dividends throughout their lives. Today, identify one difficult conversation you've been avoiding, and commit to initiating it this week. Pray for wisdom, choose a good time and setting, and approach it with humility and love.

Day 16: The Courage to Rest

Word of the Day: SABBATH

Scripture Reading: Exodus 20:8-10 (NIV)
"Remember the Sabbath day by keeping it holy. Six days you shall labor and do all your work, but the seventh day is a Sabbath to the LORD your God. On it you shall not do any work, neither you, nor your son or daughter..."

Reflection:

In a culture that glorifies busyness and equates rest with laziness, one of the most countercultural and courageous things you can do is rest. God didn't suggest rest; He commanded it. He built it into the rhythm of creation and modeled it Himself. Yet many fathers feel guilty about resting, believing their worth is tied to their output. But rest isn't the opposite of work; it's the completion of work. It's an act of trust that declares, "God is in control, and I don't have to be." Your value isn't determined by your productivity.

Courageous rest means setting aside regular time—daily, weekly, and seasonally—to stop working, to be still, to enjoy God's presence, to connect with your family, to engage in activities that restore your soul. It means protecting your Sabbath from the encroachment of work and endless to-do lists. It means modeling for your children that rest is not only acceptable but essential, that God designed our bodies and souls to require regular renewal, that pushing yourself to exhaustion isn't noble—it's unsustainable.

When you rest, you're more patient, more present, more creative, and more effective. You're also teaching your children a crucial life skill: the ability to cease striving, to trust God, to find their identity in something other than achievement.

Today, evaluate your rest patterns. Are you getting adequate sleep? Are you taking a weekly Sabbath? Make one change that moves you toward healthier rest, and model this for your family.

Day 17: Courage in Conflict Resolution

Word of the Day: RECONCILE

Scripture Reading: Matthew 5:23-24 (ESV)
"So if you are offering your gift at the altar and there remember that your brother has something against you, leave your gift there before the altar and go. First be reconciled to your brother, and then come and offer your gift."

Reflection:

Conflict is inevitable in family life. You will disagree with your wife. You will clash with your children. Tensions will arise. The question isn't whether conflict will occur but how you'll respond when it does. Many men handle conflict in unhealthy extremes: they either explode in anger, using their size and voice to dominate, or they withdraw completely, avoiding confrontation and letting resentment build. But courageous fatherhood requires a third way—healthy conflict resolution that seeks understanding, pursues reconciliation, and models Christlike humility and grace.

Healthy conflict resolution begins with self-awareness and self-control. It means recognizing when you're becoming angry and choosing to take a break rather than saying things you'll regret. It means listening to understand rather than listening to respond. It means acknowledging valid points even when you disagree. It means being willing to apologize when you're wrong and to forgive when you've been wronged. It means teaching your children that disagreement doesn't mean disconnection, that conflict can actually strengthen bonds when handled well.

Jesus prioritized reconciliation so highly that He said it should take precedence even over worship. When there's unresolved conflict in your home, it affects everything. Today, if there's unresolved conflict with anyone in your family, have the courage to initiate reconciliation. Go to them, acknowledge your part, listen to their perspective, and work toward resolution. Model for your children what it looks like to pursue peace actively.

Day 18: The Courage to Dream with Your Children

Word of the Day: VISION

Scripture Reading: Proverbs 29:18 (KJV)
"Where there is no vision, the people perish: but he that keepeth the law, happy is he."

Reflection:

One of the most powerful gifts you can give your children is the courage to dream—to imagine possibilities, to pursue their God-given passions, to believe that their lives can make a difference. But this gift requires courage from you first. It requires you to resist imposing your unfulfilled dreams on them or limiting their dreams to what seems safe or practical. It requires you to listen to their hearts, to discern their unique gifts and callings, to encourage them to pursue excellence in areas that matter to them, even if those areas differ from what you would have chosen.

Dreaming with your children means having conversations about their future that go beyond just career and college. It means helping them discover their unique design—their strengths, passions, and values. It means exposing them to diverse experiences and opportunities. It means teaching them to set goals, work hard, persevere through obstacles, and learn from failure. It means praying with them about God's calling on their lives and helping them discern His voice amid all the other voices competing for their attention. It means being their biggest cheerleader while also being their honest counselor.

Your belief in your children's potential can be the difference between them pursuing their dreams and settling for mediocrity. Today, have a conversation with each of your children about their dreams. Ask them what they're passionate about, what they hope to accomplish, what kind of person they want to become. Listen without judgment, encourage without controlling, and speak vision over their lives.

Day 19: Courage to Lead Family Worship

Word of the Day: WORSHIP

Scripture Reading: Psalm 78:4-7 (NIV)
"We will not hide them from their descendants; we will tell the next generation the praiseworthy deeds of the LORD, his power, and the wonders he has done... so the next generation would know them, even the children yet to be born, and they in turn would tell their children. Then they would put their trust in God and would not forget his deeds but would keep his commands."

Reflection:

Leading your family in worship is one of the most significant responsibilities and privileges of fatherhood, yet it's also one of the most neglected. Many fathers delegate spiritual leadership to their wives, to the church, or to no one at all. But God has called you to be the spiritual leader of your home, to create rhythms that point your family toward Him, to establish a legacy of faith passed down through generations. This doesn't require you to be a theologian or a worship leader. It simply requires intentionality about creating space for your family to encounter God together.

Family worship can take many forms — reading a Bible story before bed, singing worship songs in the car, having a weekly devotional time, sharing testimonies around the dinner table, or serving together. The specific form matters less than the consistency and authenticity. Your children need to see that faith isn't just something you practice on Sunday morning but something that permeates every aspect of life.

When you lead family worship, you're not just teaching your children about God — you're introducing them to Him. You're creating memories and establishing patterns that will shape their faith for a lifetime. If you haven't been leading family worship, start today. Choose one simple practice and commit to doing it consistently. Don't let perfection be the enemy of progress.

Day 20: The Courage to Celebrate

Word of the Day: JOY

Scripture Reading: Nehemiah 8:10 (NIV)
"Do not grieve, for the joy of the LORD is your strength."

Reflection:

In the midst of all the serious responsibilities of fatherhood —
providing, protecting, disciplining, teaching — it's easy to forget
the importance of celebration and joy. But a home without
laughter, without fun is a home that misses a crucial aspect of
God's design for family. God is not a stern taskmaster who
demands constant seriousness; He is a Father who delights in His
children, who celebrates with them, who created a world full of
beauty, pleasure, and joy. Your children need to see this side of
you.

Courageous celebration means being intentional about creating
moments of joy in your family. It means celebrating birthdays
with enthusiasm, marking milestones with special traditions,
creating family rituals that everyone looks forward to. It means
being willing to be silly, to play, to laugh at yourself, to enter your
children's world of imagination and fun. It means noticing and
celebrating the small victories — a good grade, a kind gesture,
progress in a difficult area, evidence of character growth. It means
creating an atmosphere in your home where joy is valued, where
laughter is frequent, where celebration is a regular part of life.

This doesn't mean ignoring problems or pretending everything is
perfect. It means choosing to focus on gratitude, to look for
reasons to celebrate, to create pockets of joy even in difficult
seasons. Today, plan one celebration for your family — it doesn't
have to be elaborate or expensive. It just needs to communicate, "I
notice you. I'm proud of you. Let's celebrate together."

Day 21: Courage to Invest in Your Marriage

Word of the Day: CHERISH

Scripture Reading: Ephesians 5:25 (ESV)
"Husbands, love your wives, as Christ loved the church and gave himself up for her."

Reflection:

One of the most important things you can do for your children is to love their mother well. Your marriage is the foundation of your family. When your marriage is strong, your children feel secure. When they see you treating their mother with love, respect, and honor, they learn what healthy relationships look like. When they witness you working through conflicts and serving each other, they develop a template for their own future relationships. When your marriage is struggling, your children feel the instability even if you think you're hiding it.

Investing in your marriage requires courage because it means being vulnerable, addressing issues rather than avoiding them, and continually choosing to love even when feelings fluctuate. It means dating your wife throughout your marriage, not just as newlyweds. It means speaking words of affirmation regularly. It means serving her sacrificially, noticing her needs, and meeting them without being asked. It means protecting your marriage from threats—whether excessive work hours, emotional affairs, pornography, or neglect. It means seeking counseling when you're stuck and learning and growing together.

Your children are watching how you treat their mother, and they're learning what love looks like in action. The greatest gift you can give your children is a strong, loving marriage. Today, do something specific to invest in your marriage—write your wife a note, plan a date night, have a meaningful conversation, serve her practically, or tell her why you're grateful for her.

Day 22: The Courage to Start Today

Word of the Day: BEGIN

Scripture Reading: Lamentations 3:22-23 (ESV)
"The steadfast love of the LORD never ceases; his mercies never come to an end; they are new every morning; great is your faithfulness."

Reflection:

Perhaps as you've read through these devotions on courage, you've felt overwhelmed by all the areas where you're falling short. Perhaps you're acutely aware of mistakes you've made, opportunities you've missed, years you've wasted. Perhaps you're thinking, "It's too late. I've already failed." But here's the beautiful truth of the Gospel: God's mercies are new every morning. Every single day is an opportunity to start fresh, to make different choices, to move in a new direction. You can't change the past, but you can change today. The courage to start — or to start over — is available to you right now.

Starting today doesn't mean overhauling everything at once. It means taking one step in the right direction. It means choosing one area where you'll be intentional, one conversation you'll initiate, one habit you'll establish. Small, consistent steps compound over time into significant transformation. Don't let the enemy paralyze you with guilt over the past or overwhelm you with the magnitude of what needs to change. Just start. Start praying with your kids tonight. Start having dinner together as a family this week. Start setting boundaries around your work hours. Start speaking words of affirmation. Start being present. Start pursuing your wife. Start leading family worship. Start whatever God is calling you to start, and trust that He will meet you in your obedience. Your children don't need a perfect father; they need a present one who is growing and moving forward. Today is the day. God's grace is sufficient. His mercies are new. The courage you need is available. Now is the time to begin.

DAYS 23-44: FORTITUDE - Enduring Strength for the Long Journey

Notes

Day 23: The Foundation of Fortitude

Word of the Day: ENDURE

Scripture Reading: James 1:2-4 (NIV)
"Consider it pure joy, my brothers and sisters, whenever you face trials of many kinds, because you know that the testing of your faith produces perseverance. Let perseverance finish its work so that you may be mature and complete, not lacking anything."

Reflection:

Courage gets you started, but fortitude keeps you going. If courage is the initial decision to step into intentional fatherhood, fortitude is the daily determination to stay the course when the journey gets difficult, when results are slow, when you're tired and discouraged, when your children push back. Fortitude is the strength to endure, to persevere, to remain faithful not just in moments of crisis but in the mundane, repetitive, often thankless daily grind of fatherhood. It's what separates fathers who start strong but fade from fathers who finish well.

James tells us to consider it joy when we face trials because trials produce perseverance, and perseverance produces maturity and completeness. Every difficult season, every challenge with your children, every financial pressure, every moment when you want to give up—these are opportunities for fortitude to be developed and demonstrated. Fortitude isn't about gritting your teeth and powering through in your own strength; it's about drawing on God's strength, day after day, choice after choice, trusting that He is working in you and through you even when you can't see the results.

Fatherhood is a marathon, not a sprint. You need more than an initial burst of enthusiasm; you need sustainable strength for the long journey. Today marks the beginning of building the fortitude that will enable you to remain faithful to your calling as a father for decades, through every season, every challenge, every test of your resolve.

Day 24: Persevering Through Toddler Years

Word of the Day: PATIENCE

Scripture Reading: Galatians 6:9 (ESV)
"And let us not grow weary of doing good, for in due season we will reap, if we do not give up."

Reflection:

If you have young children, you know that the toddler and preschool years can be exhausting. The constant needs, the interrupted sleep, the repetitive questions, the messes, the tantrums — it can wear down even the most patient father. These years require tremendous fortitude because the demands are relentless and the rewards are often delayed. You're investing enormous amounts of time and energy into little people who can't yet appreciate what you're doing, who will likely not remember most of these sacrificial moments. It's easy to grow weary, to check out emotionally, to leave the heavy lifting to your wife, to count down the years until they're older and "easier."

But here's what you need to know: these years matter immensely. The foundation you're laying now — the security you're providing, the love you're demonstrating, the presence you're offering — is shaping your children's brains, their attachment styles, their sense of safety in the world. Every diaper you change, every book you read, every time you get down on the floor to play — these are not wasted efforts. They are investments that will pay dividends for a lifetime. Your children may not remember these specific moments, but they will carry with them the deep, subconscious knowledge that they were loved, that they were valued, that their father was present.

Don't grow weary of doing good. The season will pass more quickly than you can imagine. Today, if you're in this season, embrace it. Choose to be present. Find joy in the small moments. And trust that your faithfulness matters more than you can see.

34

Day 25: Fortitude in the Teen Years

Word of the Day: STEADFAST

Scripture Reading: Proverbs 22:6 (NIV)
"Start children off on the way they should go, and even when they are old they will not turn from it."

Reflection:

If the toddler years test your physical endurance, the teenage years test your emotional and spiritual fortitude. Adolescence is a season of profound change — physically, emotionally, socially, and spiritually. Your children are forming their identities, testing boundaries, questioning values, and seeking independence. They may push you away even as they desperately need you. They may reject the values you've taught even as they're watching to see if you'll remain consistent. This season requires fortitude because it's easy to take their behavior personally, to give up on relationship, to become either overly controlling or completely disengaged.

But your teenagers need you now more than ever. They need you to remain steadfast — consistent in your values, unwavering in your love, persistent in your pursuit of relationship even when they push back. They need you to give them appropriate independence while maintaining appropriate boundaries. They need you to listen without lecturing, to guide without controlling, to stay connected even when connection is difficult. Remember that their behavior is often driven by developmental changes and social pressures, not by a rejection of you. The foundation you laid in earlier years is still there, even when it seems buried under teenage rebellion.

Your job is to remain faithful, to keep showing up, to keep demonstrating love, trusting that the seeds you've planted will eventually bear fruit. Don't give up on your teenagers. Stay engaged. Stay consistent. Stay loving. Your steadfast presence during these turbulent years will make a difference that may not be apparent until they're adults looking back with gratitude.

Day 26: Resilience After Failure

Word of the Day: RECOVER

Scripture Reading: Proverbs 24:16 (ESV)
"For the righteous falls seven times and rises again, but the wicked stumble in times of calamity."

Reflection:

You will fail as a father. You will lose your temper when you should have remained calm. You will miss important moments because of work demands. You will say things you regret. You will make decisions that turn out to be wrong. You will disappoint your children. You will fall short of your own standards and God's standards. The question isn't whether you'll fail—you will. The question is what you'll do after you fail. Will you wallow in guilt? Will you become defensive and blame others? Or will you demonstrate the fortitude to acknowledge your failure, learn from it, make amends, and get back up?

Fortitude includes resilience—the ability to recover from setbacks, to keep going even after you've fallen. The righteous person isn't someone who never falls; it's someone who falls and rises again. Your children need to see this modeled. They need to see that failure isn't final, that mistakes are opportunities for growth, that character is built in how we respond to imperfection.

When you fail, acknowledge it honestly. Apologize to those you've hurt. Seek God's forgiveness and grace. Learn from what went wrong. And then get back up and keep going. Don't let failures define you or derail you. God's grace is sufficient. His mercies are new every morning.

The enemy wants to use your failures to paralyze you with shame. But God wants to use them to develop humility, dependence on Him, and resilience. If you're carrying guilt over past failures, bring them to God, receive His forgiveness, make amends where necessary, and move forward with renewed commitment and hope.

36

Day 27: Persevering Through Financial Hardship

Word of the Day: PROVISION

Scripture Reading: Philippians 4:19 (NIV)
"And my God will meet all your needs according to the riches of his glory in Christ Jesus."

Reflection:

Financial hardship is one of the most stressful challenges a father can face. Whether it's job loss, unexpected expenses, mounting debt, or simply the struggle to make ends meet, financial pressure can feel overwhelming. It can affect your sense of identity as a provider, your confidence as a leader, and your relationships. The temptation is to panic, make desperate decisions, work excessive hours at the expense of family time, or withdraw emotionally out of shame. But financial hardship is an opportunity to demonstrate fortitude — to trust God's provision, lead your family with faith rather than fear, and model contentment even in difficult circumstances.

Fortitude during financial hardship means being honest with your family about the situation while also communicating confidence in God's faithfulness. It means making necessary sacrifices without complaining. It means working diligently while trusting that your worth isn't determined by your income. It means being creative and resourceful and accepting help when offered without letting pride get in the way. It means teaching your children about contentment, gratitude, and the difference between wants and needs. These seasons teach dependence on God, resilience, and the truth that joy and security don't come from material abundance. Years from now, your children may remember not what they didn't have but what they learned about faith and faithfulness. Today, take one practical step — create a budget, have an honest conversation with your wife, seek counsel, or spend time in prayer.

Day 28: The Fortitude to Keep Learning

Word of the Day: TEACHABLE

Scripture Reading: Proverbs 1:5 (ESV)
"Let the wise hear and increase in learning, and the one who understands obtain guidance."

Reflection:

One mark of fortitude is the willingness to remain teachable throughout your life. Many men reach a point where they think they've learned enough, where they become set in their ways, where they resist new information or different perspectives. But effective fatherhood requires ongoing learning and growth. Your children are constantly changing, culture is constantly shifting, and you need to keep growing in wisdom, knowledge, and understanding to lead your family well.

Remaining teachable means reading books about parenting, marriage, and spiritual growth. It means listening to podcasts, attending conferences, or taking courses that help you develop as a father and leader. It means seeking mentorship from older, wiser fathers who have successfully navigated the stages you're entering. It means being open to feedback from your wife about areas where you can improve. It means learning from your mistakes rather than repeating them. It means staying current with the challenges your children are facing—understanding social media, knowing what's happening in their schools, being aware of cultural trends that are shaping their worldview. It means being willing to change your approach when something isn't working rather than stubbornly insisting on doing things the way you've always done them.

The moment you stop learning is the moment you start becoming irrelevant and ineffective. Your children need a father who is growing, who models lifelong learning and development. Today, identify one area where you need to grow as a father, and take one step toward learning.

Day 29: Enduring Your Wife's Difficult Season

Word of the Day: SUPPORT

Scripture Reading: 1 Peter 3:7 (ESV)
"Likewise, husbands, live with your wives in an understanding way, showing honor to the woman as the weaker vessel, since they are heirs with you of the grace of life, so that your prayers may not be hindered."

Reflection:

Your wife will go through difficult seasons—postpartum depression, health challenges, grief, stress from caring for aging parents, hormonal changes, or exhaustion from managing a household and raising children. During these times, she may not function at her normal capacity. She may be emotionally fragile, physically depleted, or mentally overwhelmed. These seasons test your fortitude because they require you to step up, carry more of the load, and provide emotional support even when you're tired.

Enduring your wife's difficult season with grace and strength is one of the most important ways you can demonstrate fortitude. It means taking on additional responsibilities without complaining or keeping score. It means being emotionally present, listening without trying to fix everything immediately. It means encouraging her to get the help she needs—whether that's medical care, counseling, or time to rest. It means speaking words of affirmation even when she feels like she's failing.

Your wife needs to know that you're with her not just in the good times but especially in the difficult times. When you support her well during hard seasons, you strengthen your marriage, demonstrate Christlike love, and create a foundation of trust that will sustain your relationship for a lifetime. Today, if your wife is going through a difficult season, ask her specifically what she needs from you, and then follow through with action.

Day 30: The Long Obedience

Word of the Day: FAITHFUL

Scripture Reading: 1 Corinthians 4:2 (ESV)
"Moreover, it is required of stewards that they be found faithful."

Reflection:

Fatherhood is what Eugene Peterson called "a long obedience in the same direction." It's not about spectacular moments or heroic acts; it's about faithful presence, day after day, year after year. It's about showing up consistently, doing the right thing repeatedly, remaining committed when it's boring, staying engaged when it's difficult. This kind of long obedience requires tremendous fortitude because our culture celebrates the spectacular and the immediate, not the steady and the sustained.

But this is exactly what your children need from you—not occasional bursts of involvement but consistent, faithful presence. They need you to be there for breakfast, not just for the big game. They need you to help with homework, not just to show up for graduation. They need you to pray with them nightly, not just during crises. They need you to model integrity in small daily choices, not just to give inspiring speeches about values. They need you to love their mother consistently, not just on anniversaries.

This long obedience is built through daily choices—the choice to be present, to be patient, to be loving, to be consistent, to be faithful. It's built through routines and rhythms that may seem mundane but that create the stable foundation your family needs.

God doesn't require you to be spectacular; He requires you to be faithful. He doesn't demand perfection; He desires consistency. Today, recommit to the long obedience. Embrace the daily routines. Trust that your faithful presence, sustained over time, is creating a legacy that will outlast your lifetime.

Day 31: Fortitude in Spiritual Warfare

Word of the Day: VIGILANT

Scripture Reading: 1 Peter 5:8-9 (NIV)
"Be alert and of sober mind. Your enemy the devil prowls around like a roaring lion looking for someone to devour. Resist him, standing firm in the faith, because you know that the family of believers throughout the world is undergoing the same kind of sufferings."

Reflection:

Make no mistake: you are in a spiritual battle for your family. The enemy is real, and he is actively working to destroy your marriage, derail your children, discourage you, divide your family, and undermine everything you're building. He attacks through cultural influences, relational conflicts, financial pressure, moral temptation, and doubt. He wants you to give up, compromise, and abandon your post as spiritual leader. Fortitude in fatherhood includes spiritual vigilance — awareness that you're in a battle and determination to stand firm against the enemy's schemes.

Spiritual fortitude means putting on the full armor of God daily — truth, righteousness, the gospel of peace, faith, salvation, the Word of God, and prayer. It means recognizing attacks for what they are and responding with spiritual weapons. It means praying protection over your family, speaking Scripture over your home, and creating spiritual disciplines that strengthen faith. It means being alert to the enemy's tactics — division, distraction, deception, discouragement — and actively resisting them. It means teaching your children about spiritual warfare, helping them recognize the enemy's lies, and equipping them with truth to stand firm. This isn't about living in fear; it's about living with awareness that the battles you face have spiritual dimensions and that you need spiritual strength to prevail. Today, take your role as spiritual protector seriously. Pray specifically for protection over each family member. Put on the armor of God intentionally, and stand firm in faith.

Day 32: Persevering Through Prodigal Seasons

Word of the Day: HOPE

Scripture Reading: Luke 15:20 (NIV)
"So he got up and went to his father. But while he was still a long way off, his father saw him and was filled with compassion for him; he ran to his son, threw his arms around him and kissed him."

Reflection:

One of the most painful tests of fortitude is watching a child walk away from faith, from family values, from the path you've tried to set them on. Whether it's rebellion, addiction, destructive relationships, or simply a rejection of everything you've taught them, having a prodigal child can break your heart and test your faith like nothing else. The temptation is to give up, to write them off, or to blame yourself and wallow in guilt. But the story of the prodigal son teaches us a different response—one that requires tremendous fortitude.

The father in Jesus's parable didn't chase after his son or try to control him. He let him go, respecting his choice even though it was painful. But he also didn't give up hope. He watched for his son's return and remained ready to receive him. When his son finally came home, he ran to meet him, embraced him, and celebrated his return.

This is the fortitude required during prodigal seasons—the strength to let go without giving up, to maintain boundaries without closing your heart, to continue praying even when you see no evidence of change. Your prodigal needs to know that no matter how far they wander, they can always come home. This doesn't mean enabling destructive behavior or pretending everything is fine. It means maintaining hope, continuing to pray, refusing to give up, and trusting that God is at work even when you can't see it.

Day 33: The Fortitude of Forgiveness

Word of the Day: RELEASE

Scripture Reading: Colossians 3:13 (NIV)
"Bear with each other and forgive one another if any of you has a grievance against someone. Forgive as the Lord forgave you."

Reflection:

Fortitude includes the strength to forgive—to release resentment, to let go of grudges, to choose reconciliation over retaliation. Your children will hurt you. They will disappoint you. They will say things in anger that cut deep. Your wife will fail you at times. Others will wrong you. The question is whether you'll have the fortitude to forgive, to release the offense, to choose relationship over being right, to extend the same grace that God has extended to you. Unforgiveness is a poison that destroys you from the inside out.

Forgiveness doesn't mean pretending the offense didn't happen or that it didn't hurt. It doesn't mean there are no consequences or that trust is automatically restored. It means choosing to release the person from the debt they owe you, to stop rehearsing the offense, to stop seeking revenge. It means entrusting justice to God and choosing to move forward in grace.

Forgiveness is an act of strength, not weakness. It takes tremendous fortitude to forgive someone who has deeply hurt you, to choose mercy over judgment, to extend grace when you feel justified in withholding it. When you model forgiveness, you create a culture of grace in your home. You teach your children that relationships are more important than being right, that redemption is always possible.

Today, if you're holding unforgiveness toward anyone in your family, make the choice to forgive. Release the poison of bitterness and open the door to healing.

Day 34: Enduring Physical Limitations

Word of the Day: ADAPT

Scripture Reading: 2 Corinthians 12:9-10 (ESV)
"But he said to me, 'My grace is sufficient for you, for my power is made perfect in weakness.' Therefore I will boast all the more gladly of my weaknesses, so that the power of Christ may rest upon me. For the sake of Christ, then, I am content with weaknesses, insults, hardships, persecutions, and calamities. For when I am weak, then I am strong."

Reflection:

Whether due to injury, illness, disability, or simply the natural aging process, you may face physical limitations that affect your ability to father the way you'd like. Perhaps you can't play sports with your kids the way you once did. Perhaps chronic pain limits your energy and patience. Perhaps a disability requires you to father differently than you imagined. These limitations can be frustrating, but they also provide an opportunity to demonstrate a different kind of strength—the strength to adapt and trust that God's power is made perfect in your weakness.

Physical limitations don't disqualify you from effective fatherhood. Your children don't need you to be superhuman; they need you to be present and engaged in whatever ways you can be. If you can't run with them, you can still listen to them. If you can't coach their team, you can still attend their games. If you can't do physically demanding activities, you can still read with them, pray with them, teach them, and love them. Your limitations also teach your children about perseverance and that a person's value isn't determined by physical abilities. Paul's thorn in the flesh became an opportunity for God's power to be displayed. Your limitations can serve the same purpose. Today, ask God to show you how to father effectively within your limitations. Focus on what you can do rather than what you can't.

Day 35: The Strength to Grieve Well

Word of the Day: LAMENT

Scripture Reading: Psalm 34:18 (NIV)
"The LORD is close to the brokenhearted and saves those who are crushed in spirit."

Reflection:

Fortitude doesn't mean suppressing emotions or pretending everything is fine when it's not. Sometimes fortitude means having the strength to grieve well—to acknowledge loss, to feel pain, to lament honestly before God, and to lead your family through seasons of sorrow with authenticity and faith. Whether you're grieving the loss of a loved one, a miscarriage, a broken dream, a child's diagnosis, or any other significant loss, your family needs you to model healthy grief. They need to see that it's okay to be sad, that faith doesn't mean denying pain, that strong men can cry, that God is present in our sorrow.

Grieving well means creating space for your family to express their emotions, to ask hard questions, and to be honest about their pain. It means not rushing the process or trying to fix everything quickly. It means bringing your lament to God, following the example of the psalmists who cried out to God with raw honesty, expressing their anguish while still clinging to faith.

Fathering Strong Insight: "Like the mighty oak that bends but doesn't break during fierce storms, fathers with fortitude grow stronger through adversity." The fortitude to grieve well—to bend without breaking, to lead your family through the valley of the shadow of death—is a profound expression of strength.

Today's Challenge: If you're currently grieving, give yourself permission to feel. Talk to your family about the person or dream you've lost. Share a memory. Shed a tear. Pray together. Show them that fortitude includes the strength to be vulnerable.

Day 36: The Marathon Mindset

Word of the Day: ENDURANCE

Scripture Reading: Hebrews 12:1-2 (NIV)
"Therefore, since we are surrounded by such a great cloud of witnesses, let us throw off everything that hinders and the sin that so easily entangles. And let us run with perseverance the race marked out for us, fixing our eyes on Jesus, the pioneer and perfecter of faith."

Reflection:

Fatherhood isn't a sprint; it's a marathon requiring resilience, patience, and unwavering commitment. The father who finishes well isn't necessarily the one who starts strong, but the one who keeps going when the path gets difficult. Marathon runners know that the race is won or lost in the middle miles—those long, unglamorous stretches where enthusiasm has faded but the end isn't yet in sight.

In fatherhood, those middle miles might be the elementary school years when everything feels routine, the teenage years when rebellion tests your resolve, or the young adult years when they're making their own choices. These are the seasons when many fathers check out emotionally, distracted by work or hobbies or disappointment. But these are precisely the seasons when your steady presence matters most.

Fathering Strong Insight: Fortitude is what carries you through sleepless nights with a newborn, challenging teenage years, and every trial in between. The marathon mindset means pacing yourself and remembering that God runs with you, strengthening you for every mile.

Today's Challenge: Identify what "mile" you're currently in as a father. Ask God for the specific endurance you need for this season. Then do one thing today that invests in the long-term relationship with your children.

Day 37: Fortitude in Your Health

Word of the Day: STEWARDSHIP

Scripture Reading: 1 Corinthians 6:19-20 (NIV)
"Do you not know that your bodies are temples of the Holy Spirit, who is in you, whom you have received from God? You are not your own; you were bought at a price. Therefore honor God with your bodies."

Reflection:

Your physical health isn't just about you—it's about your capacity to serve your family for the long haul. Fortitude includes the discipline to care for your body, to make choices today that will allow you to be present and active with your children and grandchildren tomorrow. This isn't about achieving a perfect physique or running marathons (unless that's your calling); it's about being a faithful steward of the body God gave you so you can fulfill the mission He's given you.

Many fathers sacrifice their health on the altar of provision, working long hours, eating poorly, and ignoring warning signs. But what good is financial provision if you're not around to enjoy your family? The fortitude to prioritize your health—to say no to that extra project, to go to bed at a reasonable hour, to exercise even when you're tired—is an investment in your family's future.

Fathering Strong Insight: Physical strength is part of the foundation. You can't lead effectively if you're constantly depleted, sick, or running on empty.

Today's Challenge: Make one specific commitment to improve your physical health. Maybe it's scheduling that doctor's appointment you've been putting off. Maybe it's committing to walk three times this week. Maybe it's going to bed 30 minutes earlier. Choose one thing and do it—not for vanity, but for stewardship.

Day 38: The Fortitude of Consistency

Word of the Day: FAITHFULNESS

Scripture Reading: Luke 16:10 (NIV)
"Whoever can be trusted with very little can also be trusted with much, and whoever is dishonest with very little will also be dishonest with much."

Reflection:

One of the most powerful expressions of fortitude is simple consistency—showing up day after day, keeping your promises, following through on commitments, maintaining your standards even when no one is watching. Consistency isn't flashy or dramatic, but it's the bedrock of trust and the foundation of security. Your kids need to know that you're the same person on Monday as you are on Sunday, that your values don't shift with your mood, that your love doesn't depend on their performance.

Consistency requires fortitude because it's hard. It's easier to be enthusiastic for a week than faithful for a year. It's easier to make grand promises than to keep small ones. But your children aren't shaped primarily by your mountaintop moments; they're shaped by your everyday choices. They're watching to see if you do what you say you'll do. They're learning whether commitments matter.

Fathering Strong Insight: Daily habits—that's where fortitude shows up. Not in occasional heroics, but in faithful consistency.

Today's Challenge: Think about one area where you've been inconsistent with your children—maybe bedtime routines, family dinners, one-on-one time, or following through on consequences. Commit to being consistent in that area for the next seven days. Write it down. Tell someone. Then do it, even when it's inconvenient.

Day 39: Persevering Through Marital Struggles

Word of the Day: COMMITMENT

Scripture Reading: Malachi 2:16 (NIV)
"'The man who hates and divorces his wife,' says the LORD, the God of Israel, 'does violence to the one he should protect,' says the LORD Almighty. So be on your guard, and do not be unfaithful."

Reflection:

Every marriage goes through difficult seasons — times when love feels more like a choice than a feeling, when communication breaks down, when you wonder if you made a mistake. These seasons require tremendous fortitude. They require the strength to keep choosing your wife when emotions have faded, to keep working on the relationship when progress feels slow, to keep believing in the covenant you made even when it's hard.

Your children are watching how you navigate these seasons. They're learning what commitment really means. The fortitude you demonstrate in your marriage — choosing to love when it's difficult, seeking counseling when you need help, fighting for your relationship instead of fighting with each other — teaches them more about love than a thousand conversations ever could.

Fathering Strong Insight: Your children are watching every interaction, learning what love looks like by observing how you treat their mother. The fortitude to persevere through marital struggles is one of the greatest gifts you can give your children.

Today's Challenge: If your marriage is struggling, take one concrete step toward healing today. Maybe it's apologizing for something specific. Maybe it's scheduling a date night. Maybe it's calling a counselor. Maybe it's simply telling your wife one thing you appreciate about her. Don't wait for her to make the first move — lead with fortitude.

Day 40: The Strength to Wait

Word of the Day: PATIENCE

Scripture Reading: Isaiah 40:31 (NIV)
"But those who hope in the LORD will renew their strength. They will soar on wings like eagles; they will run and not grow weary, they will walk and not be faint."

Reflection:

Some of the hardest moments in fatherhood are the waiting seasons — waiting for a child to mature, waiting for a prodigal to return, waiting for a prayer to be answered, waiting for God to move. Waiting requires a unique kind of fortitude because it feels passive, like you're not doing anything. But biblical waiting isn't passive; it's active trust. It's choosing to hope when circumstances suggest despair. It's continuing to pray when you don't see results. It's maintaining faith when the timeline doesn't match your expectations.

The strength to wait well means resisting the temptation to force outcomes or manipulate situations. It means continuing to be faithful in your role even when you can't see the fruit of your labor. It means believing that God is working even when you can't see evidence of it. This kind of waiting — patient, hopeful, faithful — requires you to trust Someone you can't see more than the circumstances you can see.

Fathering Strong Insight: When fortitude and faith combine, they produce the strength to wait — not with resignation, but with hope.

Today's Challenge: Identify one situation where you're waiting for God to move. Instead of trying to force a solution, commit to active waiting — continuing to pray, continuing to be faithful, continuing to trust God's timing.

Day 41: Fortitude in Disappointment

Word of the Day: HOPE

Scripture Reading: Romans 5:3-5 (NIV)
"Not only so, but we also glory in our sufferings, because we know that suffering produces perseverance; perseverance, character; and character, hope. And hope does not put us to shame, because God's love has been poured out into our hearts through the Holy Spirit, who has been given to us."

Reflection:

Fatherhood includes disappointments—children who make choices you wouldn't make, dreams that don't materialize, expectations that aren't met. Maybe your son didn't make the team. Maybe your daughter is struggling academically. Maybe your child has rejected the faith you've tried to instill. These disappointments can crush your spirit if you let them, or they can become opportunities to demonstrate fortitude and model resilience.

The fortitude to handle disappointment well means grieving what you hoped for while still embracing what is. It means continuing to love and lead even when outcomes don't match your desires. Your children need to see you handle disappointment with grace, to watch you process pain without becoming bitter, to observe you trusting God even when life doesn't go according to plan.

Fathering Strong Insight: When disappointment comes—and it will—fortitude combined with faith allows you to find meaning in the struggle and hope in the midst of pain.

Today's Challenge: Think about a current disappointment in your fatherhood journey. Instead of dwelling on what isn't, thank God for what is. Write down three things you're grateful for, then ask God to help you respond with grace.

Day 42: The Fortitude of Self-Control

Word of the Day: DISCIPLINE

Scripture Reading: Proverbs 25:28 (NIV)
"Like a city whose walls are broken through is a person who lacks self-control."

Reflection:

Self-control is fortitude turned inward — the strength to govern your own impulses, emotions, appetites, and reactions. It's the ability to do what's right even when you feel like doing something else. It's choosing the long-term good over the short-term pleasure. It's managing your anger instead of exploding. It's controlling your tongue instead of saying something you'll regret. Your children are learning how to manage their own impulses by watching how you manage yours.

A father without self-control is like a city without walls — vulnerable to attack, unable to protect what matters most. But a father who demonstrates self-control shows his children what strength really looks like. It's not the strength to dominate others; it's the strength to master yourself.

Fathering Strong Insight: Self-control is the fortitude that keeps you from losing your temper during sleepless nights, from saying something destructive during challenging teenage years, from making impulsive decisions during trials.

Today's Challenge: Identify one area where you struggle with self-control — maybe it's your temper, eating habits, screen time, or words. Ask God for the fortitude to exercise self-control in that area today. When tempted, pause, pray, and choose the harder right over the easier wrong.

Day 43: Enduring Seasons of Doubt

Word of the Day: PERSEVERANCE

Scripture Reading: Mark 9:24 (NIV)
"Immediately the boy's father exclaimed, 'I do believe; help me overcome my unbelief!'"

Reflection:

Even the strongest fathers experience seasons of doubt—doubt about your abilities, your decisions, whether your efforts matter, even doubt about your faith. These seasons require special fortitude because you're fighting internal questions, not just external circumstances. The temptation is to hide your doubts and fake confidence you don't feel. But fortitude in seasons of doubt means being honest about your struggles while continuing to move forward in faith.

The father in Mark 9 gives us a beautiful example. He brought his son to Jesus for healing but wasn't sure it would work. Instead of pretending to have perfect faith, he was honest: "I do believe; help me overcome my unbelief!" That's fortitude—acknowledging your doubt while still choosing to trust, admitting your weakness while still seeking God's strength. Your children don't need you to have perfect faith; they need you to have authentic faith that perseveres through doubt.

Fathering Strong Insight: Faith provides the foundation upon which we build our legacy as fathers. Even when that faith is imperfect and mixed with doubt, it's still the foundation. Fortitude means building on it even when you can't see the full structure yet.

Today's Challenge: If you're experiencing doubt, be honest about it. Talk to God. Share it with a trusted friend. Then pray: "I do believe; help me overcome my unbelief!" Take the next faithful step.

Day 44: The Reward of Fortitude

Word of the Day: LEGACY

Scripture Reading: Galatians 6:9 (NIV)
"Let us not become weary in doing good, for at the proper time we will reap a harvest if we do not give up."

Reflection:

Fortitude isn't just about enduring difficulty; it's about enduring toward something—a harvest, a reward, a legacy. The promise of Scripture is clear: if you don't give up, you will reap. The father who perseveres through the sleepless nights, the challenging years, the seasons of doubt—that father will see fruit. Maybe not immediately. Maybe not in the timeline you expected. But at the proper time, you will reap a harvest if you do not give up.

This is the hope that sustains fortitude. You're not just surviving; you're building. You're not just enduring; you're investing. Every moment of perseverance, every choice to keep going when you wanted to quit—all of it matters. All of it is creating a legacy. Your children may not appreciate your fortitude now, but they will. The character you're developing through perseverance will shape not just your life, but generations to come. The harvest is coming. Don't give up before you see it.

Fathering Strong Insight: This legacy is built through fortitude— the daily choice to keep going, keep loving, keep leading, keep trusting, even when it's hard.

Today's Challenge: Take a moment to envision the harvest you're working toward. What kind of adults do you hope your children become? What legacy do you hope to leave? Write it down. Then recommit to the fortitude required to see that harvest come to fruition. Remember: you will reap if you do not give up.

DAYS 45-66: FAITH - The Foundation That Holds Everything Together

Notes

Day 45: Faith as Your Foundation

Word of the Day: TRUST

Scripture Reading: Proverbs 3:5-6 (NIV)
"Trust in the LORD with all your heart and lean not on your own understanding; in all your ways submit to him, and he will make your paths straight."

Reflection:

Faith is the foundation upon which everything else in fatherhood is built. Without faith, courage becomes recklessness, fortitude becomes stubbornness, and love becomes sentimentality. But with faith—a deep-rooted belief in God's character, His promises, and His purposes—everything changes. Faith provides the moral compass that guides your decisions, the hope that sustains you through trials, and the meaning that transforms everyday moments into eternal investments.

In the journey of fatherhood, we all face moments that test our limits—moments when we don't know what to do, when our wisdom runs out, when our strength fails. Faith provides the deep-rooted belief in something greater than ourselves, a source of strength that carries us through our toughest days. It's the confidence that God is working even when we can't see it, that He's faithful even when we're not, that His plans are better than ours even when we don't understand them.

Fathering Strong Insight: When you lead your family with faith, you're not just teaching religious concepts; you're showing them how to navigate life with confidence in God's goodness, wisdom, and power. You're modeling what it means to trust Someone bigger than yourself.

Today's Challenge: Identify one area of your fatherhood where you've been leaning on your own understanding instead of trusting God. Surrender it to God today. Pray specifically, asking Him to guide you and committing to trust His direction even if it doesn't match your plan.

Day 46: Teaching Faith Through Your Story

Word of the Day: TESTIMONY

Scripture Reading: Psalm 78:4 (NIV)
"We will not hide them from their descendants; we will tell the next generation the praiseworthy deeds of the LORD, his power, and the wonders he has done."

Reflection:

One of the most powerful ways to build faith in your children is to tell them your story—how you came to faith, how God has worked in your life, how He's answered prayers, how He's carried you through difficult times. Your testimony is living proof that God is real and active. When your children hear how God has worked in your life, it builds their confidence that He'll work in theirs too.

Many fathers hesitate to share their spiritual journey because they think their story isn't dramatic enough or because they're embarrassed about their past. But your children don't need a perfect testimony; they need an authentic one. They need to hear about your struggles and victories, your doubts and breakthroughs, your failures and redemption. They need to know that the faith you're teaching them is personal, tested, and proven in your own life.

Fathering Strong Insight: Stories matter. Your story matters. Don't underestimate the power of sharing your faith journey with your children. It's one of the most valuable inheritances you can give them.

Today's Challenge: Share one specific story with your children about how God has worked in your life. Make it personal, make it real, and help them see that the God you're teaching them about is the same God who's been faithful to you.

Day 47: The Prayer Life of a Father

Word of the Day: INTERCESSION

Scripture Reading: 1 Thessalonians 5:16-18 (NIV)
"Rejoice always, pray continually, give thanks in all circumstances; for this is God's will for you in Christ Jesus."

Reflection:

Prayer is the most powerful tool you have as a father. Through prayer, you access divine wisdom for decisions, supernatural strength for challenges, and God's intervention in situations beyond your control. When you pray for your children, you're inviting God into their lives in ways you never could through your own efforts. You're asking the Creator of the universe to work in their hearts, to protect them from harm, to guide their steps, to draw them to Himself.

A father's prayer life doesn't have to be complicated or eloquent. It can be as simple as brief prayers throughout the day — thanking God for your children, asking for wisdom in a specific situation, interceding for a struggle they're facing, praying protection over them as they leave the house. What matters isn't the length or eloquence of your prayers; what matters is the consistency and sincerity of your communication with God about your family.

Fathering Strong Insight: Through stories like Jacob's — a father who prays with his children before school each morning — we see how faith provides a moral compass, fosters hope and resilience, and helps find meaning in life's challenges. Prayer is how you access that compass, foster that hope, and find that meaning.

Today's Challenge: Commit to praying for each of your children by name today. Pray specifically — not just general blessings, but prayers tailored to their unique personalities, struggles, and seasons. Even five minutes of consistent prayer will transform your fatherhood.

Day 48: Faith in the Mundane

Word of the Day: FAITHFULNESS

Scripture Reading: Colossians 3:23 (NIV)
"Whatever you do, work at it with all your heart, as working for the Lord, not for human masters."

Reflection:

Faith isn't just for the big moments — the crises, the major decisions, the dramatic interventions. Faith is also for the mundane, everyday moments of fatherhood: changing diapers, packing lunches, helping with homework, driving to practice. These ordinary moments can feel insignificant, but when you approach them with faith — seeing them as opportunities to serve God by serving your family — they become sacred. They become acts of worship.

Most of fatherhood is mundane. Most days are just showing up, doing the work, being present, staying faithful. But this is where faith matters most — in the ordinary, unglamorous, repetitive tasks that no one applauds. When you change that diaper as an act of service to God, when you help with that homework as an expression of your faith — you're building something eternal in the midst of the temporal.

Fathering Strong Insight: Daily habits — that's where faith shows up most consistently. Not in occasional spiritual highs, but in faithful presence in the mundane moments.

Today's Challenge: Choose one mundane task you'll do today as a father — something ordinary and repetitive. Before you do it, pause and offer it to God as an act of worship. Ask Him to help you see it not as a chore, but as a sacred opportunity to serve your family and honor Him. Then do it with excellence and joy.

Day 49: Trusting God with Your Children's Future

Word of the Day: SURRENDER

Scripture Reading: Jeremiah 29:11 (NIV)
"'For I know the plans I have for you,' declares the LORD, 'plans to prosper you and not to harm you, plans to give you hope and a future.'"

Reflection:

One of the hardest aspects of faith in fatherhood is trusting God with your children's future. You can't control who they'll become, who they'll marry, what career they'll choose, or what decisions they'll make. You can guide, teach, model, and pray — but ultimately, you have to surrender them to God's care and trust that His plans for them are better than yours.

Trusting God with your children's future doesn't mean being passive or uninvolved. It means doing your part faithfully — teaching them, training them, loving them, praying for them — while recognizing that the outcome is in God's hands. It means releasing the anxiety that comes from trying to control everything and resting in the confidence that God is sovereign, good, and faithful.

Fathering Strong Insight: "Whether you're a new dad holding your first child or navigating the complex waters of raising teenagers, Fathering Strong offers the blueprint needed to build an unshakeable foundation of faith and purpose in your family."

Today's Challenge: Write down your biggest fear or worry about your children's future. Then physically or symbolically surrender it to God — maybe by praying over it and tearing up the paper. Every time that worry resurfaces, remind yourself that God's plans for your children are better than yours, and choose to trust Him.

Day 50: Faith That Asks Hard Questions

Word of the Day: HONESTY

Scripture Reading: Psalm 13:1-2 (NIV)
"How long, LORD? Will you forget me forever? How long will you hide your face from me? How long must I wrestle with my thoughts and day after day have sorrow in my heart?"

Reflection:

Authentic faith doesn't mean having all the answers or never questioning God. Sometimes faith means bringing your hardest questions to God — the "why" questions, the "how long" questions, the "where are you" questions. The psalms are filled with these kinds of honest, raw prayers. David and other psalmists didn't pretend everything was fine when it wasn't. They brought their confusion, frustration, pain, and questions directly to God. And God didn't reject them for their honesty; He met them in their struggle.

Your children need to see this kind of faith — faith that's honest about doubt, that wrestles with hard questions, that doesn't have all the answers but still chooses to trust. When you model authentic faith, you give them permission to bring their own questions and doubts to God instead of hiding them or walking away from faith altogether.

Fathering Strong Insight: "Faith provides a moral compass, fosters hope and resilience, and helps find meaning in life's challenges." Part of finding meaning in challenges is being honest about how hard they are and trusting God even when answers don't come immediately.

Today's Challenge: If you have hard questions for God, don't hide them. Write them down. Pray them honestly. Bring them to God with confidence that He can handle your questions and that honest wrestling is part of authentic faith. If appropriate, share one of your questions with your children and model what it looks like to trust God in the midst of uncertainty.

Day 51: Building a Family Altar

Word of the Day: WORSHIP

Scripture Reading: Joshua 24:15 (NIV)
"But if serving the LORD seems undesirable to you, then choose for yourselves this day whom you will serve, whether the gods your ancestors served beyond the Euphrates, or the gods of the Amorites, in whose land you are living. But as for me and my household, we will serve the LORD."

Reflection:

Throughout Scripture, fathers built altars—physical places where they worshiped God, made sacrifices, and marked significant moments in their spiritual journey. While we don't build physical altars today, we can create spiritual "altars" in our homes—regular times and spaces where our families encounter God together. This might be family devotions, bedtime prayers, Sunday morning worship preparation, or mealtime thanksgiving. Whatever form it takes, a family altar is a declaration: "As for me and my household, we will serve the LORD."

Building a family altar doesn't require perfection or extensive biblical knowledge. It just requires intentionality—creating regular rhythms where your family focuses on God together. The specific form matters less than the consistent practice.

Fathering Strong Insight: "Family worship can take many forms— reading Scripture at breakfast, praying before bed, or having spiritual conversations during everyday moments. Don't let perfection be the enemy of progress. Just start."

Today's Challenge: If you don't already have a regular family worship practice, start one today. Maybe just read one verse and pray together at dinner, or pray with each child at bedtime. The goal isn't perfection; it's consistency.

Day 52: Faith in God's Provision

Word of the Day: PROVISION

Scripture Reading: Matthew 6:31-33 (NIV)
"So do not worry, saying, 'What shall we eat?' or 'What shall we drink?' or 'What shall we wear?' For the pagans run after all these things, and your heavenly Father knows that you need them. But seek first his kingdom and his righteousness, and all these things will be given to you as well."

Reflection:

Financial anxiety is one of the greatest threats to a father's peace and faith. The pressure to provide can become overwhelming, leading to workaholism, stress, and a constant sense of inadequacy. But Jesus calls us to a different way — a way of faith that trusts God to provide what we need as we seek first His kingdom.

Faith in God's provision means making financial decisions based on biblical principles rather than cultural pressures. It means being generous even when resources are tight. It means living within your means and teaching your children that contentment comes from God, not from possessions. This kind of faith is countercultural, but it leads to peace, freedom, and a powerful testimony.

Fathering Strong Insight: Your faith in God's provision — demonstrated through how you earn, spend, save, and give — teaches your children profound lessons about trust, contentment, and stewardship.

Today's Challenge: Evaluate your financial life through the lens of faith. Are you trusting God or trusting your paycheck? Identify one way you can demonstrate faith in God's provision — maybe through increased giving, simplified living, or releasing a financial worry to God in prayer.

Day 53: The Faith to Forgive

Word of the Day: GRACE

Scripture Reading: Ephesians 4:32 (NIV)
"Be kind and compassionate to one another, forgiving each other, just as in Christ God forgave you."

Reflection:

Faith and forgiveness are inseparably linked. When you truly understand how much God has forgiven you, it changes how you respond when others — including your children — need forgiveness from you. Faith enables you to extend grace instead of holding grudges, to release offenses instead of keeping score. This is especially important in fatherhood because your children will disappoint you, disobey you, and hurt you. How you respond in those moments will shape their understanding of grace, forgiveness, and God's character.

Forgiveness doesn't mean there are no consequences or that you ignore serious issues. It means you don't hold the offense against them, you don't bring it up repeatedly, you don't let it define your relationship. When your children see you forgive quickly and completely, they learn that mistakes don't define them, that relationship is more important than being right, that grace is real and available.

Fathering Strong Insight: "The first time I had to admit to my kids that I'd made a mistake, my pride wanted to defend my actions. But courage meant saying, 'I was wrong, and I'm sorry.' That moment actually strengthened our relationship more than a thousand 'perfect' parenting moments." Forgiveness flows both ways — you forgiving them, and them forgiving you.

Today's Challenge: Is there an offense you're holding against one of your children? Release it today. Tell them you forgive them (if appropriate), or simply release it in your heart and choose not to bring it up again.

Day 54: Faith That Celebrates

Word of the Day: JOY

Scripture Reading: Nehemiah 8:10 (NIV)
"Nehemiah said, 'Go and enjoy choice food and sweet drinks, and send some to those who have nothing prepared. This day is holy to our Lord. Do not grieve, for the joy of the LORD is your strength.'"

Reflection:

Faith isn't just about enduring hardship; it's also about celebrating goodness. The joy of the Lord is your strength—not just grim determination, but genuine joy in God's goodness, His blessings, His faithfulness. A father who leads with faith creates a home where joy is present, where God's goodness is celebrated, where gratitude is expressed. This doesn't mean ignoring difficulties, but choosing to see and celebrate God's goodness even in the midst of challenges.

Your children need to see that faith produces joy, not just duty. They need to experience a home where laughter is common, where celebrations happen, where God's blessings are noticed and appreciated. When you lead with joyful faith, you show them that following God isn't a burden—it's a delight. You demonstrate that the Christian life is about relationship and abundant life. You create memories of joy that will draw them back to faith when life gets hard.

Fathering Strong Insight: While courage, fortitude, and faith are crucial, there's one virtue that fuels them all: love. As 1 Corinthians 16:14 reminds us, "Do everything in love." And love celebrates. Love finds reasons to rejoice. Faith-filled fatherhood includes the joy of celebrating God's goodness with your family.

Today's Challenge: Plan a celebration with your family—it doesn't have to be elaborate. Maybe it's celebrating a small victory, marking a milestone, or simply celebrating God's faithfulness. Create a moment of joy and gratitude.

66

Day 55: Teaching Your Children to Pray

Word of the Day: INSTRUCTION

Scripture Reading: Luke 11:1 (NIV)
"One day Jesus was praying in a certain place. When he finished, one of his disciples said to him, 'Lord, teach us to pray, just as John taught his disciples.'"

Reflection:

Your children won't automatically know how to pray; they need to be taught. And the best teacher is you—not because you're an expert, but because you're their father. When you pray with them and teach them to pray, you're giving them a tool they'll use for the rest of their lives. You're showing them how to communicate with God, bring their needs to Him, express gratitude, and intercede for others.

Teaching your children to pray doesn't require theological expertise. It just requires authenticity and consistency. Pray with them at bedtime. Pray before meals. Pray when they're worried or scared. Let them hear you pray—not perfectly crafted prayers, but honest conversations with God. Teach them simple frameworks like ACTS (Adoration, Confession, Thanksgiving, Supplication) or encourage them to talk to God like they'd talk to a loving father. The goal isn't eloquence; it's connection.

Fathering Strong Insight: "Praying out loud as a father doesn't require eloquence or theological precision. It just requires authenticity—honest communication with God that your children can witness and learn from. When they hear you pray, they learn that prayer is real, that God listens, that you depend on Him."

Today's Challenge: Pray out loud with each of your children today. If they're young, help them pray by asking: "What do you want to thank God for? What do you need help with?" If they're older, invite them to pray and then you pray after them.

Day 56: Faith in the Waiting Room

Word of the Day: ENDURANCE

Scripture Reading: Psalm 27:13-14 (NIV)
"I remain confident of this: I will see the goodness of the LORD in the land of the living. Wait for the LORD; be strong and take heart and wait for the LORD."

Reflection:

Some of the hardest tests of faith happen in waiting rooms—literal ones when your child is sick or injured, and metaphorical ones when you're waiting for God to answer a prayer or move in your child's life. These waiting seasons test your faith because you can't see what God is doing, you can't control the outcome, and you can't speed up the process. All you can do is wait, trust, and remain faithful. But this is where faith grows deepest—not in dramatic moments of immediate answers, but in the long, quiet seasons of faithful waiting.

Faith in the waiting room means continuing to trust God's goodness even when you can't see evidence of it. It means believing He's working even when circumstances suggest otherwise. It means maintaining hope when despair would be easier. It means modeling for your children what it looks like to trust God in the unknown and hold onto hope when the situation is unclear.

Fathering Strong Insight: "Faith provides the deep-rooted belief in something greater than ourselves, a source of strength that carries us through our toughest days." In the waiting room, that deep-rooted belief is what sustains you.

Today's Challenge: If you're currently in a "waiting room" season, recommit to faithful waiting today. Instead of trying to force an outcome or giving in to despair, choose to trust God's timing. Pray specifically, asking for the faith to wait well and the strength to remain hopeful.

Day 57: The Faith to Let Go

Word of the Day: RELEASE

Scripture Reading: Luke 15:20 (NIV)
"So he got up and went to his father. But while he was still a long way off, his father saw him and was filled with compassion for him; he ran to his son, threw his arms around him and kissed him."

Reflection:

One of the most difficult expressions of faith is letting go — allowing your children to make their own choices, even when you disagree with those choices. This doesn't mean abandoning your role as a father or approving of destructive decisions. It means recognizing that at some point, your children must own their faith, their choices, and their lives. You can't force them to follow God or live according to your values. All you can do is love them, pray for them, and trust God to work in their lives in ways you can't.

The father of the prodigal son demonstrates this kind of faith. He didn't chase after his son or try to control him. He let him go, even though it broke his heart. But he also watched for his return, ready to welcome him home with open arms. This is the faith required in fatherhood — the faith to release your children to God's care, to trust that He loves them even more than you do, and to remain ready to welcome them home whenever they return.

Fathering Strong Insight: God loves them more than you do. Trust Him to reach them in ways you can't.

Today's Challenge: If you have a child who's making choices you disagree with, evaluate whether you're trying to control them or trusting God with them. Pray specifically for that child, then release them to God's care, trusting that He's faithful even when they're not.

Day 58: Faith That Serves

Word of the Day: SERVICE

Scripture Reading: Mark 10:45 (NIV)
"For even the Son of Man did not come to be served, but to serve, and to give his life as a ransom for many."

Reflection:

Faith isn't just about what you believe; it's about how you live. One of the clearest expressions of authentic faith is service—using your time, energy, and resources to meet the needs of others. When you serve your family, church, community, and those in need, you're demonstrating that your faith is real and compels you to love others practically. Your children need to see this faith in action—faith that demonstrates love through service.

Serving as a family is one of the most powerful ways to build faith in your children. When you serve together—whether helping a neighbor, volunteering at church, or meeting a community need—you're showing them that faith is active, that following Jesus means serving others. You're also creating shared experiences that build family identity and values. Years from now, your children will remember serving alongside you, and those memories will shape their understanding of what it means to live out their faith.

Fathering Strong Insight: Service is one of the most tangible ways to demonstrate faith. It's faith with hands and feet.

Today's Challenge: Plan a service opportunity for your family. It doesn't have to be elaborate—maybe helping an elderly neighbor with yard work, preparing a meal for someone in need, or volunteering at a local ministry. Involve your children and talk about why you're serving—because God has served you, and faith compels you to serve others.

Day 59: The Faith to Speak Truth

Word of the Day: CONVICTION

Scripture Reading: Ephesians 4:15 (NIV)
"Instead, speaking the truth in love, we will grow to become in every respect the mature body of him who is the head, that is, Christ."

Reflection:

Faith gives you the conviction to speak truth to your children — truth about God, right and wrong, consequences, and life. In a culture that increasingly rejects absolute truth and moral standards, your children need you to be a voice of clarity, speaking truth with conviction while also speaking it in love. This requires faith because it's countercultural, often unpopular, and sometimes creates conflict. But your children need you to be anchored in truth, not swayed by cultural trends or popular opinion.

Speaking truth in love means being both clear and compassionate. It means not compromising on biblical standards while also not being harsh or judgmental. It means addressing difficult topics — sexuality, identity, morality, faith — with honesty and grace. It means being willing to have uncomfortable conversations because you love your children too much to leave them confused about what's true.

Fathering Strong Insight: "Faith provides a moral compass, fosters hope and resilience, and helps find meaning in life's challenges." That moral compass is rooted in truth — God's truth revealed in Scripture. Your faith gives you the conviction to speak that truth clearly and the wisdom to speak it lovingly.

Today's Challenge: Identify one area where your children need to hear truth from you — maybe about a cultural issue, a moral question, or a faith topic. Don't avoid the conversation because it's uncomfortable. Pray for wisdom, then speak truth in love, helping them understand what God's Word says about it.

71

Day 60: Faith in God's Timing

Word of the Day: PATIENCE

Scripture Reading: Ecclesiastes 3:1 (NIV)
"There is a time for everything, and a season for every activity under the heavens."

Reflection:

One of the most challenging aspects of faith is trusting God's timing. You want your children to mature spiritually—now. You want them to make wise decisions—now. You want to see the fruit of your parenting—now. But God's timing rarely matches ours. Faith means trusting that God's timing is perfect, even when it feels slow to you.

This is especially difficult when you see your children struggling or making poor choices. You want immediate change, instant maturity, quick resolution. But spiritual growth doesn't work that way. It's a process, often a slow one, with setbacks and detours. Faith in God's timing means continuing to pray, continuing to love, continuing to teach—while trusting that God is working even when you can't see evidence of it. It means believing that the seeds you're planting today will bear fruit in the future, even if you don't see the harvest immediately.

Fathering Strong Insight: "Whether you're a new dad holding your first child or navigating the complex waters of raising teenagers, Fathering Strong offers the blueprint needed to build an unshakeable foundation of faith and purpose in your family." That foundation is built over time, through faithful consistency. Trust the process.

Today's Challenge: Identify one area where you're frustrated with the timing. Instead of trying to force faster results, surrender the timing to God. Pray specifically, asking Him to work in His perfect timing and asking for the faith to trust Him while you wait.

Day 61: The Faith to Bless

Word of the Day: BLESSING

Scripture Reading: Numbers 6:24-26 (NIV)
"The LORD bless you and keep you; the LORD make his face shine on you and be gracious to you; the LORD turn his face toward you and give you peace."

Reflection:

Throughout Scripture, fathers blessed their children—speaking words of identity, destiny, favor, and faith over them. This wasn't just a nice tradition; it was a powerful spiritual act that shaped how children saw themselves and their future. You have the same opportunity. When you speak blessing over your children— affirming their identity in Christ, declaring God's purposes for their lives, expressing your love and belief in them—you're exercising faith. You're calling forth what God has placed in them, even before it's fully visible.

Blessing your children doesn't require a formal ceremony. It can happen in everyday moments—at bedtime, before school, during difficult seasons, or just because. It might sound like: "I see God's hand on your life." "You have a gift for encouraging others." "I believe God has great plans for you." "I'm proud of the person you're becoming." These words, spoken with faith and love, have power to shape your children's identity and future.

Fathering Strong Insight: "Dreaming with your children means having conversations about their future, their gifts, and God's purposes for their lives. It means speaking vision over them, believing in them, and helping them see possibilities when they can't yet see it themselves." Blessing is one way you speak that vision.

Today's Challenge: Speak a specific blessing over each of your children today. Look them in the eye, put your hand on their shoulder, and speak words of faith, identity, and destiny over them. Make this a regular practice.

Day 62: Faith That Perseveres in Prayer

Word of the Day: PERSISTENCE

Scripture Reading: Luke 18:1 (NIV)
"Then Jesus told his disciples a parable to show them that they should always pray and not give up."

Reflection:

Some prayers are answered quickly; others require persistent, long-term faith. You may pray for years for a child's salvation, for healing in a relationship, for breakthrough in a struggle, for change in a situation. The temptation is to give up when answers don't come quickly, to assume God isn't listening or doesn't care. But Jesus taught that we should always pray and not give up. Persistent prayer is an expression of faith—faith that God hears, faith that He cares, faith that He will answer in His perfect timing.

Persistent prayer doesn't mean nagging God or trying to manipulate Him into doing what you want. It means continuing to bring your requests to Him, continuing to trust Him with the outcome, continuing to believe that He's working even when you can't see it. It means praying the same prayer day after day, year after year if necessary, because you believe God is faithful and His timing is perfect. This kind of persistent, faithful prayer is one of the most powerful things you can do as a father.

Fathering Strong Insight: "Through prayer, you access divine wisdom for decisions, supernatural strength for challenges, and God's intervention in situations beyond your control." But sometimes that intervention requires persistent prayer over time. Don't give up. Keep praying. Keep believing. Keep trusting.

Today's Challenge: Identify one prayer you've been praying for a long time without seeing an answer. Instead of giving up, recommit to persistent prayer today. Write down that prayer request and commit to praying it daily for the next 30 days. Trust that God hears, that He cares, and that He will answer in His perfect timing.

Day 63: The Faith to Admit You Don't Know

Word of the Day: HUMILITY

Scripture Reading: Proverbs 3:7 (NIV)
"Do not be wise in your own eyes; fear the LORD and shun evil."

Reflection:

Faith includes the humility to admit when you don't know something—when you don't have the answer, when you're not sure what to do, when you need help. Many fathers feel pressure to have all the answers, but this isn't faith; it's pride. True faith acknowledges your limitations and points to God as the source of wisdom. When you tell your children "I don't know, but let's find out together" or "I'm not sure, but let's pray about it," you're modeling authentic faith that depends on God rather than human wisdom.

Admitting you don't know doesn't undermine your authority; it actually strengthens it because it shows your children that your confidence isn't in yourself, but in God. It teaches them that seeking wisdom is a strength not a weakness, that depending on God is the wisest thing anyone can do. It also creates opportunities to learn and grow alongside your children, to seek God's wisdom together, to discover truth as a family.

Fathering Strong Insight: Seeking help might mean finding a mentor, joining a men's group, or seeing a counselor. Seeking help isn't giving up; it's gearing up for victory. The same humility that seeks help from others also admits when you don't have all the answers.

Today's Challenge: The next time your child asks you a question you don't know the answer to, resist the urge to fake it. Instead, say "I don't know, but that's a great question. Let's find out together." Then actually follow through—look it up, ask someone who knows, or pray about it together.

Day 64: Faith in the Small Things

Word of the Day: FAITHFULNESS

Scripture Reading: Luke 16:10 (NIV)
"Whoever can be trusted with very little can also be trusted with much, and whoever is dishonest with very little will also be dishonest with much."

Reflection:

Faith isn't just for the big moments — the major decisions, the crises, the dramatic interventions. Faith is also demonstrated in the small things — keeping your word about small promises, being honest in small matters, showing integrity in small decisions, being faithful in small responsibilities. These small acts of faithfulness may seem insignificant, but they're actually the foundation for everything else. Your children are watching to see if your faith is real in the everyday moments, not just the Sunday moments.

When you keep your promise to play catch even though you're tired, when you tell the truth even when a small lie would be easier, when you return the extra change the cashier gave you by mistake — you're demonstrating that your faith is real. You're showing your children that integrity matters in small things, that faithfulness is a way of life, that your relationship with God affects every area of your life.

Fathering Strong Insight: Modeling integrity in the small things means doing what's right even when no one is watching, even when the wrong thing is easier or more convenient. You're always teaching, whether you intend to or not.

Today's Challenge: Pay attention to the small choices you make today. Choose to be faithful in those small things. Keep a small promise. Tell the truth in a small matter. Let your children see that your faith affects every area of your life.

Day 65: The Faith to Hope

Word of the Day: HOPE

Scripture Reading: Romans 15:13 (NIV)
"May the God of hope fill you with all joy and peace as you trust in him, so that you may overflow with hope by the power of the Holy Spirit."

Reflection:

Hope is faith directed toward the future. It's the confident expectation that God is working, that He will be faithful, that the best is yet to come. As a father, you need hope—hope that your efforts matter, hope that your children will turn out well, hope that God is working even when you can't see it. Without hope, fatherhood becomes a burden of anxiety and fear. But with hope rooted in faith, fatherhood becomes an adventure of trust and expectation.

Your children desperately need you to be a source of hope. They need you to believe in them when they don't believe in themselves. They need you to see potential when they only see failure. They need you to maintain hope when circumstances are discouraging. When you lead with hope, you create an atmosphere of faith in your home—a belief that God is good, that He's working, that the future is bright because He holds it.

Fathering Strong Insight: "Faith provides a moral compass, fosters hope and resilience, and helps find meaning in life's challenges." Hope sustains you through challenges and enables you to see beyond present circumstances to future possibilities.

Today's Challenge: Identify one area where you've lost hope—maybe regarding a child's struggle or your own effectiveness as a father. Ask God to renew your hope in that area. Then speak hope to your family—express confidence in God's faithfulness and belief in your children's potential.

Day 66: Faith That Finishes Well

Word of the Day: LEGACY

Scripture Reading: 2 Timothy 4:7 (NIV)
"I have fought the good fight, I have finished the race, I have kept the faith."

Reflection:

The ultimate test of faith isn't how you start, but how you finish. Many fathers start strong—full of enthusiasm and commitment. But the true measure of faith is whether you're still faithful at the end—still loving your family, still following God, still living with integrity. Faith that finishes well is faith that endures through every season, every challenge, every test.

Finishing well means staying faithful in the later seasons of fatherhood—when your children are grown, when your role shifts from active parenting to supportive presence, when you're investing in grandchildren. It means continuing to grow spiritually, continuing to serve, continuing to point others to Christ. The legacy you leave isn't just what you did when your children were young; it's who you are throughout your entire life.

Fathering Strong Insight: "More than just another parenting guide, this book serves as an invaluable resource for any father determined to create a legacy that will impact generations to come." That legacy is built through faith that endures from beginning to end. Don't just start well—finish well.

Today's Challenge: Think about the legacy you want to leave. What do you want your children and grandchildren to remember about you? Write down your vision for finishing well, then identify one thing you need to do today to move toward that vision. Commit to faith that endures from start to finish.

DAYS 67-90: LOVE - The Virtue That Fuels Everything Else

Notes

Day 67: Love as the Foundation

Word of the Day: LOVE

Scripture Reading: 1 Corinthians 16:14 (NIV)
"Do everything in love."

Reflection:

While courage, fortitude, and faith are crucial, there's one virtue that fuels them all: love. Love is the motivation behind your courage, the purpose of your fortitude, the expression of your faith. Without love, courage becomes recklessness, fortitude becomes stubbornness, and faith becomes empty religion. But with love, everything changes. Love transforms duty into delight, obligation into opportunity, sacrifice into joy.

Love in fatherhood isn't primarily a feeling; it's a choice, a commitment, an action. It's choosing to serve your family even when you're tired. It's choosing to be patient even when you're frustrated. It's choosing to forgive even when you're hurt. It's choosing to sacrifice even when it's costly. This kind of love—sacrificial, unconditional, persistent—is what your family needs most from you.

Fathering Strong Insight: "While courage, fortitude, and faith are crucial, there's one virtue that fuels them all: love. As 1 Corinthians 16:14 reminds us, 'Do everything in love.'" Everything. Every interaction with your children. Every decision you make. Every word you speak. Let love be the motivation, the method, and the message.

Today's Challenge: Evaluate your interactions with your family today through the lens of love. Choose one interaction—maybe discipline, a conversation, a routine task—and consciously do it in love, letting love shape your attitude, your words, and your actions.

Day 68: The Love That Shows Up

Word of the Day: PRESENCE

Scripture Reading: Matthew 28:20 (NIV)
"And surely I am with you always, to the very end of the age."

Reflection:

One of the most powerful expressions of love is simply showing up—being present physically, emotionally, and mentally. Your children don't need a perfect father; they need a present father. They need you to be there for the big moments and the small ones, the exciting times and the boring ones, the celebrations and the struggles.

Showing up means putting down your phone when your child wants to talk. It means attending their games, recitals, and events even when you're tired. It means being home for dinner instead of always working late. It means listening when they share about their day instead of half-listening while thinking about something else. This kind of presence—consistent, engaged, attentive—communicates love more powerfully than any words ever could.

Fathering Strong Insight: "The courage to be present requires fighting against the distractions that pull you away—work demands, personal hobbies, digital devices, mental preoccupation—and choosing to give your focused attention on the people who matter most." Presence is love in action.

Today's Challenge: Be fully present with your family today. Put away your phone during family time. Make eye contact when your children talk to you. Ask questions and actually listen to the answers. Give them your undivided attention, even if just for 15 minutes. Show them that they're worth your full presence.

Day 69: Love That Disciplines

Word of the Day: CORRECTION

Scripture Reading: Hebrews 12:6 (NIV)
"Because the Lord disciplines the one he loves, and he chastens everyone he accepts as his son."

Reflection:

Love doesn't mean permissiveness; it means caring enough to correct. When you discipline your children, you're not being mean—you're being loving. You're teaching them that actions have consequences, that boundaries exist for their protection, that character matters more than temporary happiness. The world will tell you that discipline is harsh, but Scripture tells us the opposite—that God disciplines those He loves, and we should follow His example.

Loving discipline requires wisdom, consistency, and self-control. It means addressing behavior promptly but not in anger. It means explaining the "why" behind the rules and always affirming your love even as you correct behavior. Your children need to know that discipline comes from love, not frustration. When discipline is rooted in love rather than anger, it builds trust rather than resentment. It teaches them that boundaries are for their protection and that your love is unconditional even when your approval is conditional.

Fathering Strong Insight: "The courage to discipline with love requires fighting against the temptation to be their friend rather than their father." Your children don't need another friend; they need a father who loves them enough to guide them and shape their character even when it's uncomfortable.

Today's Challenge: If there's a behavior issue you've been avoiding, commit to addressing it today. Prepare your heart first— pray for wisdom, check your motives, calm your emotions—then address it with love, clarity, and appropriate consequences.

Day 70: Loving Your Wife Well

Word of the Day: CHERISH

Scripture Reading: Ephesians 5:25, 28-29 (NIV)
"Husbands, love your wives, just as Christ loved the church and gave himself up for her... In this same way, husbands ought to love their wives as their own bodies. He who loves his wife loves himself. After all, no one ever hated their own body, but they feed and care for their body, just as Christ does the church."

Reflection:
One of the most important ways you love your children is by loving their mother. Your marriage is the foundation of your family, the model your children will follow when they form their own relationships. When you love your wife well—when you serve her, honor her, pursue her, cherish her—you're teaching your sons how to treat women and your daughters what to expect from men.

Loving your wife well means prioritizing your marriage even in the busy seasons of parenting. It means dating her intentionally, communicating regularly, and serving sacrificially. It means speaking well of her to your children, defending her when they're disrespectful, supporting her parenting decisions, and presenting a united front. Your children are watching how you treat their mother, and they're learning what love looks like.

Fathering Strong Insight: The way you speak to her, serve her, and prioritize her will shape their understanding of love and relationships more than any conversation you could have with them.

Today's Challenge: Do something today that demonstrates love for your wife in a way your children can observe—helping with dinner, speaking words of affirmation, or simply holding her hand.

Day 71: The Love of Affection

Word of the Day: TENDERNESS

Scripture Reading: Luke 15:20 (NIV)
"But while he was still a long way off, his father saw him and was filled with compassion for him; he ran to his son, threw his arms around him and kissed him."

Reflection:
Physical affection is a powerful expression of love that many fathers struggle to give, especially to their sons. But your children—all of them—need your affectionate touch. They need hugs, high-fives, pats on the back, and physical presence. They need to know that you're not just proud of what they do but delighted in who they are. The father in the parable of the prodigal son didn't just welcome his son home with words; he ran to him, threw his arms around him, and kissed him. This is the picture of God's love for us, and it's the model for how we should love our children.

Affection communicates acceptance, belonging, and unconditional love in ways that words alone cannot. It builds emotional security and strengthens your bond with your children. If you didn't receive affection from your own father, breaking this pattern might feel awkward at first. But your discomfort is a small price to pay for your children's emotional health. Start small—a hand on the shoulder, a side hug—and build from there.

Fathering Strong Insight: "Your children desperately need your affection. They need to know they're loved not just in theory but in tangible, physical ways. Your willingness to push through discomfort will pay dividends for generations."

Today's Challenge: Give each of your children meaningful physical affection today. For younger children, this might be wrestling or cuddling. For older children, it might be a hug or a hand on the shoulder. Don't let the day end without physical expressions of your love.

Day 72: Love That Listens

Word of the Day: ATTENTION

Scripture Reading: James 1:19 (NIV)
"My dear brothers and sisters, take note of this: Everyone should be quick to listen, slow to speak and slow to become angry."

Reflection:
One of the most loving things you can do for your children is to truly listen to them—not just hear their words while thinking about your response, but genuinely listen to understand their hearts, their perspectives, and their feelings. Listening communicates value. It says, "You matter. Your thoughts matter. Your feelings matter." In our fast-paced, distraction-filled culture, the gift of your full attention is one of the most precious things you can give.

Loving listening means putting down your phone, turning off the TV, making eye contact, and giving your full presence to the conversation. It means asking follow-up questions, reflecting back what you hear, validating their emotions even when you don't agree with their conclusions, and resisting the urge to immediately fix, correct, or lecture. Sometimes your children don't need solutions; they need to be heard. This kind of listening builds trust, opens doors for deeper conversations, and creates a relationship where they'll come to you with the big things because you've consistently listened to the small things.

Fathering Strong Insight: "The courage to be present requires fighting against distractions, setting aside your agenda, and giving focused attention on the people who matter most." Listening is one of the most practical ways to be present. It's love in action.

Today's Challenge: Have a conversation with each of your children today where your only goal is to listen and understand, not to teach, correct, or fix. Ask open-ended questions and practice listening without interrupting or looking at your phone. Just listen.

Day 73: Sacrificial Love

Word of the Day: SACRIFICE

Scripture Reading: John 15:13 (NIV)
"Greater love has no one than this: to lay down one's life for one's friends."

Reflection:
Love always costs something. It costs time, energy, comfort, convenience, money, and sometimes even dreams. Sacrificial love means putting your children's needs above your wants, their development above your comfort, their future above your present convenience. It means getting up with a sick child even though you have an early meeting. It means missing the game to attend their recital. It means spending money on their education instead of your hobby.

Jesus modeled the ultimate sacrificial love by literally laying down His life for us. While we may never be called to die physically for our children, we're called to die to ourselves daily—to our selfishness, our convenience, our comfort—for their sake. This is the essence of fatherhood: laying down your life so they can thrive. The beautiful paradox is that in losing your life for them, you find it. In sacrificing for them, you gain something far more valuable than anything you gave up.

Fathering Strong Insight: Sacrificial love is what transforms intentions into impact. It's the daily choice to put their needs above your wants.

Today's Challenge: Identify one specific sacrifice you need to make for your children—something that will cost you time, money, comfort, or convenience—and commit to making it. Make the sacrifice joyfully, knowing that love always costs something.

Day 74: Love That Forgives

Word of the Day: GRACE

Scripture Reading: Colossians 3:13 (NIV)
"Bear with each other and forgive one another if any of you has a grievance against someone. Forgive as the Lord forgave you."

Reflection:
Your children will disappoint you. They'll disobey, disrespect, and make choices that hurt you and themselves. In those moments, they need to experience your forgiveness—not cheap grace that ignores sin, but costly grace that acknowledges the offense and chooses to forgive anyway. When you forgive your children, you're giving them a picture of how God forgives us. You're teaching them that mistakes don't define them, that relationship is more important than being right, that love covers a multitude of sins.

Forgiveness doesn't mean there are no consequences. It means that after the consequence is served, the offense is truly released. You don't bring it up again in future arguments. You don't hold it over their heads. You forgive as you've been forgiven—completely, freely, and repeatedly. This creates a home where grace abounds, where people can fail and get back up, where love is stronger than mistakes.

Fathering Strong Insight: "The first time I admitted to my kids that I'd made a mistake, my pride wanted to defend my actions. But courage meant saying, 'I was wrong, and I'm sorry.' That moment actually strengthened our relationship more than a thousand 'perfect' parenting moments." Forgiveness flows both ways and requires humility and love.

Today's Challenge: If one of your children has disappointed you recently, choose to truly forgive them today—releasing the offense and moving forward in love.

Day 75: Love That Celebrates

Word of the Day: JOY

Scripture Reading: Zephaniah 3:17 (NIV)
"The Lord your God is with you, the Mighty Warrior who saves.
He will take great delight in you; in his love he will no longer
rebuke you, but will rejoice over you with singing."

Reflection:
God doesn't just tolerate us; He delights in us, rejoices over us,
celebrates us. This is the kind of love your children need to
experience from you—love that celebrates who they are, not just
what they accomplish. Love that notices the small victories,
acknowledges the effort even when the outcome isn't perfect, and
finds reasons to celebrate regularly. In a world that constantly
criticizes and compares, your home should be a place where your
children are celebrated.

Celebration doesn't require big events or expensive gifts. It's found
in the everyday moments when you notice something good and
call it out. "I saw how patient you were with your sister today—
that was really mature." "You worked so hard on that project, and
it shows." These moments of celebration build your children's
confidence, reinforce positive behavior, and create a home
atmosphere of joy and encouragement.

Fathering Strong Insight: "The courage to celebrate means being
intentional about noticing the good, expressing your delight, and
creating moments that say, 'I see you. I'm proud of you. I'm
grateful for you.'" Don't wait for perfect report cards or
championship games. Celebrate the everyday faithfulness, the
small improvements, the unique qualities that make each child
special.

Today's Challenge: Find something specific to celebrate about
each of your children today. Celebrate it verbally, and if possible,
do something special to mark it—their favorite dessert, a special
activity, or a small gift.

Day 76: Love in the Mundane

Word of the Day: FAITHFULNESS

Scripture Reading: Luke 16:10 (NIV)
"Whoever can be trusted with very little can also be trusted with much, and whoever is dishonest with very little will also be dishonest with much."

Reflection:
Most of fatherhood isn't made up of dramatic moments or major milestones. It's made up of mundane, repetitive, ordinary moments — making lunches, helping with homework, driving to practice, reading bedtime stories. These moments can feel insignificant, but they're actually where love is most powerfully expressed. Faithfulness in the small things builds trust, creates security, and shapes character. Your consistent presence in the ordinary moments matters more than your occasional presence in the extraordinary ones.

Love in the mundane means showing up day after day, even when it's boring, even when you're tired. It means being faithful in the little things — keeping your promises, following through on commitments, being consistent in discipline, and showing up for the everyday moments that no one else will remember but your children will never forget. This is where legacy is built — not in the big moments that everyone sees, but in the small moments that only your family experiences.

Fathering Strong Insight: Faith isn't just for the big moments — the crises, the major decisions, the dramatic interventions. Faith is most often expressed in the small, daily choices to trust God and obey His Word. The same is true for love.

Today's Challenge: Embrace the mundane tasks of fatherhood today with joy and intentionality. Let your children see that you don't just love them in the big moments; you love them in the ordinary ones too.

Day 77: Love That Protects

Word of the Day: GUARDIAN

Scripture Reading: Psalm 121:7-8 (NIV)
"The Lord will keep you from all harm—he will watch over your life; the Lord will watch over your coming and going both now and forevermore."

Reflection:
One of your primary responsibilities as a father is to protect your children—physically, emotionally, spiritually, and mentally. This means being aware of dangers they might not see, setting boundaries they might not understand, and sometimes saying no to things they desperately want. Protective love isn't controlling or fearful; it's wise and vigilant.

Physical protection is the most obvious—keeping them safe from harm and teaching them about dangers. But emotional and spiritual protection are equally important. This means monitoring what they consume through media, knowing who their friends are, being aware of what they're exposed to online, and creating a home environment where they're safe to be themselves. It also means protecting them from your own anger and unresolved pain. Sometimes the greatest threat to your children's wellbeing is an unhealed father.

Fathering Strong Insight: "Standing against cultural currents doesn't mean being angry or rigid. It means being thoughtfully engaged, helping your children navigate cultural trends through the lens of biblical truth, and having the courage to set boundaries that align with God's truth." Protection requires discernment, courage, and the willingness to be unpopular.

Today's Challenge: Evaluate one area where your children might need more protection—whether it's their screen time, their friendships, their schedule, or their exposure to certain influences. Have a conversation with your wife about it, pray for wisdom, and take one concrete step to provide better protection.

Day 78: Love That Serves

Word of the Day: HUMILITY

Scripture Reading: Mark 10:45 (NIV)
"For even the Son of Man did not come to be served, but to serve, and to give his life as a ransom for many."

Reflection:
Jesus, the King of Kings, demonstrated His love through service. He washed His disciples' feet, healed the sick, fed the hungry, and ultimately gave His life for us. This is the model for fatherhood — love expressed through humble service. Serving your family isn't beneath you; it's the highest expression of your leadership. When you serve your children — when you help with dishes, clean up messes, make meals, do laundry, help with projects — you're demonstrating that love is active, that leadership means service, that greatness is found in humility.

Your children need to see you serve, not just direct. They need to see you roll up your sleeves and do the unglamorous work of family life. This teaches them that no task is beneath them, that service is noble, that love is expressed through action.

Fathering Strong Insight: Your children are watching to see if your faith makes a difference in how you treat people, handle money, respond to difficulty, and serve others. Service is faith in action. It's love made visible.

Today's Challenge: Look for opportunities to serve your family today in practical, tangible ways. Do a chore that's usually someone else's responsibility. Help with something without being asked. Serve in a way that costs you something — time, energy, or convenience. Do it joyfully, without expecting recognition or thanks.

Day 79: Love That Speaks Life

Word of the Day: AFFIRMATION

Scripture Reading: Proverbs 18:21 (NIV)
"The tongue has the power of life and death, and those who love it will eat its fruit."

Reflection:
Your words have tremendous power in your children's lives. Words of affirmation, encouragement, blessing, and vision build their confidence, shape their identity, and give them courage to become who God created them to be. Conversely, words of criticism, comparison, or contempt can wound deeply and last for years. Love speaks life. It chooses words carefully, speaks truth with grace, and blesses abundantly.

Speaking life to your children means being intentional about what you say and how you say it. Catch them doing things right and call it out. Speak to their potential, not just their performance. Affirm their character, not just their accomplishments. Say "I love you" regularly, "I'm proud of you" specifically, and "I believe in you" consistently. Your children will internalize the words you speak over them. They'll hear your voice in their heads for the rest of their lives. Make sure you're giving them words worth remembering—words that build up, encourage, inspire, and bless.

Fathering Strong Insight: "Blessing your children doesn't require a formal ceremony or perfect words. It simply requires a father who sees the potential God has placed in them and is willing to speak that vision over their life."

Today's Challenge: Speak specific words of life over each of your children today. Tell them something you appreciate about their character, something you see God doing in their life, or something you believe about their future.

Day 80: Love That Pursues

Word of the Day: INITIATIVE

Scripture Reading: Luke 19:10 (NIV)
"For the Son of Man came to seek and to save the lost."

Reflection:
Jesus didn't wait for us to come to Him; He pursued us. He left heaven, took on flesh, and died for us while we were still sinners. This is the kind of love your children need from you—love that pursues, that takes initiative, that actively seeks them out. Pursuing love means being intentional about spending time with each child individually, asking about their lives, entering their world, and showing interest in what matters to them.

Pursuit looks different at different ages. With young children, it might mean getting down on the floor to play with them or reading their favorite book for the hundredth time. With teenagers, it might mean learning about their music, asking thoughtful questions about their opinions, or inviting them to do something they enjoy. The key is that you're taking the initiative. You're showing them that they're worth pursuing, that relationship with them is a priority for you.

Fathering Strong Insight: "The courage to be present requires fighting against distractions, setting aside your agenda, and giving focused attention on the people who matter most." Pursuit is presence with intention.

Today's Challenge: Pursue each of your children today with intentional one-on-one time. It doesn't have to be long—even 15 minutes of focused attention can be powerful. Ask them about something specific in their life, do an activity they enjoy, or simply sit with them and talk.

Day 81: Love That Teaches

Word of the Day: WISDOM

Scripture Reading: Deuteronomy 6:6-7 (NIV)
"These commandments that I give you today are to be on your hearts. Impress them on your children. Talk about them when you sit at home and when you walk along the road, when you lie down and when you get up."

Reflection:
One of the most loving things you can do for your children is to teach them—not just academic knowledge, but life wisdom, biblical truth, practical skills, and godly character. Your children need you to be their primary teacher, the one who helps them understand the world, navigate relationships, make decisions, and follow God. This teaching happens both formally and informally—in planned conversations and spontaneous moments, in structured lessons and everyday experiences.

Teaching your children means being intentional about passing on what you know, what you've learned, and what you believe. It means having conversations about God, character, relationships, money, work, and everything that matters. It means using everyday moments as teaching opportunities—the drive to school, the dinner table, the bedtime routine. It means not just telling them what to do but explaining why, helping them understand the principles behind the rules.

Fathering Strong Insight: "Courageous fatherhood means recognizing that you're always teaching, whether you intend to or not. Your children are learning from your example, your words, your reactions, and your choices. The question isn't whether you're teaching them; it's what you're teaching them."

Today's Challenge: Identify one important life lesson or biblical truth you want to teach your children, and find a way to teach it today. Don't just tell them; help them understand and apply it.

Day 82: Love That Lets Go

Word of the Day: RELEASE

Scripture Reading: Proverbs 22:6 (NIV)
"Start children off on the way they should go, and even when they are old they will not turn from it."

Reflection:
One of the hardest expressions of love is letting go—releasing your children to make their own choices, experience their own consequences, and become their own people. From the moment they're born, you're preparing them to leave. Every stage of parenting involves gradually releasing control, giving them more freedom, and trusting them with more responsibility. This is terrifying because you know they'll make mistakes, and you want to protect them from pain. But love sometimes means stepping back and letting them learn, even when it's hard to watch.

Letting go doesn't mean abandoning them or becoming uninvolved. It means shifting from control to influence, from directing to advising, from managing to mentoring. It means trusting the foundation you've built, believing in the character you've instilled, and having faith that God will continue the work you've started. The goal of parenting isn't to keep your children dependent on you forever; it's to raise them to be independent, godly adults who can stand on their own faith and make wise decisions.

Fathering Strong Insight: "Whether you're a new dad holding your first child or navigating the complex waters of raising teenagers, Fathering Strong offers the blueprint needed to build an unshakeable foundation of faith and purpose in your family." That foundation is what allows you to eventually let go.

Today's Challenge: Identify one area where you need to give your children more freedom or responsibility. Take one step toward healthy release today.

Day 83: Love That Hopes

Word of the Day: EXPECTATION

Scripture Reading: 1 Corinthians 13:7 (NIV)
"[Love] always protects, always trusts, always hopes, always perseveres."

Reflection:
Love hopes. It believes the best about people, expects good things, and maintains optimism even in difficult circumstances. Your children need you to hope for them — to believe in their potential even when they're struggling, to see who they're becoming even when they're not there yet, to maintain faith in their future even when their present is messy. Hope isn't naive optimism that ignores reality; it's faith-filled expectation that God is at work, that growth is happening, that the story isn't over yet.

When you hope for your children, you're giving them something to live up to. You're speaking vision over their lives and believing in them even when they don't believe in themselves. This doesn't mean ignoring problems or pretending everything is fine. It means addressing issues while maintaining hope, correcting behavior while believing in character, and dealing with the present while keeping faith in the future. Your hope becomes their hope. Your belief in them becomes the foundation for their belief in themselves.

Fathering Strong Insight: Hope is faith directed toward your children's future. It's the conviction that God has good plans for them, that He's not finished with them yet, that their best days are still ahead.

Today's Challenge: Write down specific hopes you have for each of your children — not just what you hope they'll accomplish, but who you hope they'll become. Share these hopes with them in an encouraging conversation.

Day 84: Love That Prays

Word of the Day: INTERCESSION

Scripture Reading: 1 Thessalonians 5:16-18 (NIV)
"Rejoice always, pray continually, give thanks in all circumstances; for this is God's will for you in Christ Jesus."

Reflection:
The most powerful way you can love your children is to pray for them. Prayer is the way you partner with God in their lives, inviting His presence, His protection, His guidance, and His work in their hearts. When you pray for your children, you're acknowledging that you can't do this alone, that they need more than you can give them, that God loves them even more than you do and has better plans for them than you could imagine. Prayer is love on its knees, interceding for the ones you love most.

Praying for your children should be a daily practice, as natural as breathing. Pray for their character, their faith, their relationships, their future, their struggles, their gifts, their protection, and their purpose. Pray with them and for them. Let them hear you pray, so they know you're bringing them before God. Your prayers are building a spiritual foundation under their lives that will hold them steady when storms come.

Fathering Strong Insight: "The courage to pray consistently for your children requires faith that God hears and acts, even when you don't see immediate results. Your prayers are never wasted — they're investments in eternity."

Today's Challenge: Set aside time today to pray specifically for each of your children. Write down your prayers if it helps you focus. Then tell your children that you prayed for them today and share one thing you prayed about.

Day 85: Love That Blesses

Word of the Day: BENEDICTION

Scripture Reading: Numbers 6:24-26 (NIV)
"The Lord bless you and keep you; the Lord make his face shine on you and be gracious to you; the Lord turn his face toward you and give you peace."

Reflection:
Throughout Scripture, fathers blessed their children—speaking words of identity, destiny, and favor over them. This wasn't just a nice tradition; it was a powerful act that shaped how children saw themselves and their future. Your blessing matters. When you speak words of affirmation, identity, and calling over your children, you're doing more than encouraging them—you're partnering with God to call forth who He created them to be.

A father's blessing doesn't require perfect words or formal language. It's the intentional act of speaking life, hope, and God's favor over your children. It's telling them who they are, whose they are, and what you see God doing in them. Your blessing can be a regular practice—at bedtime, before big moments, or just in everyday conversations. Make it a habit to bless your children with your words.

Fathering Strong Insight: "Your children are listening for your voice to tell them who they are. Make sure they hear blessing, not just correction. Make sure they know you see the good God is growing in them."

Today's Challenge: Speak a blessing over each of your children today. Place your hand on their head or shoulder, look them in the eye, and speak words of identity and calling over them. Tell them what you see in them and what you believe God is doing in their lives.

Day 86: Love That Remembers

Word of the Day: LEGACY

Scripture Reading: Psalm 78:4-7 (NIV)
"We will not hide them from their descendants; we will tell the next generation the praiseworthy deeds of the Lord, his power, and the wonders he has done."

Reflection:
Your children need to know their story—not just their own story, but the story of your family, your faith, and God's faithfulness through generations. When you share memories, tell family stories, and recount how God has worked in your life, you're giving your children a heritage. You're showing them that they're part of something bigger than themselves, that God has been faithful before and will be faithful again.

Create traditions that help your family remember. Celebrate milestones. Mark spiritual moments. Tell stories of God's provision, protection, and presence. Take photos, keep journals, create rituals that anchor your family's identity in God's faithfulness. These memories become the foundation your children stand on when their own faith is tested.

Fathering Strong Insight: "The stories you tell become the legacy you leave. Make sure your children know the stories of God's faithfulness—in Scripture, in your family, and in your own life."

Today's Challenge: Share a story with your children about a time when God was faithful to you or your family. Make it specific and personal. Help them see that the God who was faithful then is faithful now.

Day 87: Love That Equips

Word of the Day: PREPARATION

Scripture Reading: 2 Timothy 3:16-17 (NIV)
"All Scripture is God-breathed and is useful for teaching, rebuking, correcting and training in righteousness, so that the servant of God may be thoroughly equipped for every good work."

Reflection:
Your job as a father isn't just to love your children—it's to equip them for life. You're preparing them to leave, to stand on their own, to make wise decisions, to follow God, to build their own families, and to impact their world. This means intentionally teaching them practical skills, spiritual disciplines, emotional intelligence, and biblical wisdom. It means letting them try, fail, learn, and grow under your guidance.

Equipping takes time and intentionality. It means teaching them how to pray, how to study Scripture, how to manage money, how to resolve conflict, how to serve others, how to work hard, and how to rest well. It means having conversations about faith, relationships, integrity, and purpose. Don't assume they'll figure it out on their own—be intentional about preparing them for what's ahead.

Fathering Strong Insight: "Courageous fatherhood means preparing your children for a future without you physically present, while ensuring they carry your values, your faith, and your love with them wherever they go."

Today's Challenge: Identify one practical or spiritual skill your children need to learn. Begin teaching them that skill this week— whether it's how to pray, how to change a tire, how to apologize well, or how to read the Bible.

Day 88: Love That Endures

Word of the Day: PERSEVERANCE

Scripture Reading: 1 Corinthians 13:7-8 (NIV)
"[Love] always protects, always trusts, always hopes, always perseveres. Love never fails."

Reflection:
Fatherhood isn't a sprint—it's a marathon. There will be seasons when your children push you away, when they make choices that break your heart, when you feel like you're failing, when you don't see the fruit of your investment. In those moments, you need love that endures. Love that doesn't give up. Love that keeps showing up, keeps praying, keeps believing, keeps hoping, even when it's hard.

Your consistent presence matters more than you know. Your refusal to quit on your children—even when they quit on themselves—reflects the love of God who never gives up on us. Enduring love doesn't mean tolerating destructive behavior, but it does mean maintaining relationship, keeping the door open, and continuing to pursue your children's hearts no matter how long it takes.

Fathering Strong Insight: "The courage to keep loving when love isn't returned, to keep investing when you don't see results, to keep showing up when it would be easier to walk away—that's the love that changes lives."

Today's Challenge: If you're in a difficult season with one of your children, recommit today to enduring love. Pray for perseverance. Take one step toward them, even if it's small. Don't give up.

Day 89: Love That Points to Jesus

Word of the Day: GOSPEL

Scripture Reading: John 14:6 (NIV)
"Jesus answered, 'I am the way and the truth and the life. No one comes to the Father except through me.'"

Reflection:
The ultimate goal of your fatherhood isn't to raise good kids—it's to point your children to Jesus. Everything you've learned over these 90 days—courage, faith, integrity, presence, discipline, love—it all points to the gospel. Your children need to see Jesus in you, hear about Jesus from you, and ultimately come to know Jesus for themselves. This is the most important thing you can do as a father.

You point your children to Jesus by living out your faith authentically, by talking about Him naturally in everyday life, by showing them what it looks like to follow Him, and by praying that the Holy Spirit would draw them to salvation. You can't save your children—only Jesus can—but you can faithfully point them to Him every single day.

Fathering Strong Insight: "Your greatest legacy isn't what your children accomplish or achieve—it's whether they know Jesus. Everything else is secondary to this one eternal priority."

Today's Challenge: Have a conversation with your children about Jesus. Share your testimony, ask about their faith, pray with them, or simply talk about what Jesus means to you. Make the gospel clear and personal.

Day 90: Love That Continues

Word of the Day: COMMITMENT

Scripture Reading: Joshua 24:15 (NIV)
"But as for me and my household, we will serve the Lord."

Reflection:
You've reached day 90, but your journey as a father doesn't end here. Everything you've learned, every challenge you've accepted, every change you've made — these aren't just exercises to complete. They're the beginning of a lifelong commitment to fathering strong. The courage, faith, and love you've been building over these 90 days need to continue every single day for the rest of your life.

Fatherhood is a calling that doesn't retire. Even when your children are grown, you're still their father. Even when they have children of their own, they still need your wisdom, your prayers, your presence, and your love. The investment you make today will echo through generations. The legacy you build will outlive you. So keep going. Keep growing. Keep loving. Keep pointing your family to Jesus.

Fathering Strong Insight: "These 90 days were never meant to be the finish line — they were meant to be the starting blocks. The real work begins now, as you take everything you've learned and live it out for the rest of your life."

Today's Challenge: Review the past 90 days. What has changed in you? What has changed in your family? Write down your commitment to continue growing as a father. Share your commitment with your wife or a trusted friend who can encourage you and hold you accountable. Then make a plan for how you'll continue to grow — whether that's re-reading these devotions, finding a mentor, joining a men's group, or simply committing to daily prayer and intentional fatherhood. This is just the beginning.

Conclusion: The Journey Continues

Congratulations. You've completed 90 days of intentional growth as a father. You've wrestled with courage, built fortitude, deepened your faith, and learned to love more fully. But as you close this book, I want you to understand something crucial: this isn't the end. It's the beginning.

Over these past three months, you've been building something—not just reading words on a page, but constructing a foundation that will support your family for generations. You've been developing the four pillars that hold up faithful fatherhood: the courage to step into your calling, the fortitude to endure through every season, the faith to trust God when your wisdom runs out, and the love that fuels everything else.

But here's what I need you to hear: these virtues aren't destinations you arrive at. They're muscles you continue to strengthen. They're habits you continue to practice. They're commitments you continue to renew, day after day, year after year, for the rest of your life.

What You've Built

Think back to Day 1. Remember the father you were when you started this journey? The fears you carried, the questions you had, the areas where you felt inadequate? Now look at where you are today. You've grown. You've changed. You've taken steps toward becoming the father God designed you to be.

Maybe you've started praying with your kids at bedtime. Maybe you've had that difficult conversation you'd been avoiding. Maybe you've set boundaries you needed to establish. Maybe you've forgiven an offense you'd been holding onto. Maybe you've simply shown up more consistently, been more present, loved more intentionally.

These aren't small things. These are the building blocks of legacy. Every prayer you've prayed, every moment you've been present, every time you've chosen courage over comfort, every act of sacrificial love — all of it matters. All of it is creating something that will outlast your lifetime.

The Reality Check

But let me be honest with you: you're going to have days when you feel like you've learned nothing. Days when you lose your temper, when you're too tired to be present, when you make the wrong call, when you fall back into old patterns. You're going to have moments when you wonder if any of this is making a difference.

In those moments, I want you to remember this truth: God's mercies are new every morning. Every single day is an opportunity to start fresh, to make different choices, to move in a new direction. You don't have to be a perfect father. You just need to be a faithful one — a man who keeps showing up, keeps growing, keeps trying, and keeps trusting God to fill in the gaps where you fall short.

The enemy wants to use your failures to paralyze you with shame, to convince you that you're not cut out for this, that you've already blown it. But God wants to use those same failures to develop humility, dependence on Him, and resilience. The difference between fathers who finish well and fathers who give up isn't perfection — it's perseverance.

Your Next Steps

So where do you go from here? How do you ensure that these 90 days become a lifestyle rather than just a season?

First, **don't stop learning**. This devotional was never meant to be your only resource. Keep reading. Keep growing. Find mentors who are further along in the journey. Join a men's group where you can be honest about your struggles. Attend conferences. Listen to podcasts. Stay teachable. The moment you think you've learned enough is the moment you start becoming ineffective.

Second, **stay accountable**. Find another father — or better yet, a small group of fathers — who will walk this journey with you. Share your struggles. Celebrate your victories. Challenge each other. Pray for each other. You weren't designed to do this alone. The fathers who thrive are the ones who have brothers in the trenches with them.

Third, **keep practicing the disciplines**. The challenges you've completed over these 90 days weren't just exercises — they were training for a lifestyle. Keep praying with your kids. Keep having one-on-one time with each child. Keep speaking words of blessing. Keep serving your wife. Keep setting boundaries. Keep showing up. These practices become powerful when they become patterns.

Fourth, **revisit this journey**. Consider going through these devotions again in six months or a year. You'll be in a different season, facing different challenges, and the same truths will speak to you in new ways. Or better yet, go through it with other fathers, discussing each day's reading together. The insights you gain in community will be even richer than what you discovered alone.

Finally, **pass it on**. As you grow as a father, look for opportunities to encourage other men in their fatherhood journey. Share what you've learned. Be honest about your struggles. Mentor younger fathers. Your experience — both your successes and your failures — can be a gift to others who are walking the path behind you.

The Legacy You're Building

Your children are watching. They're learning what it means to be a man, what it means to follow God, what it means to love a family. They're forming their understanding of who God is based largely on who you are. They're developing their capacity for courage, fortitude, faith, and love by observing yours.

This is both sobering and inspiring. Sobering because the weight of that responsibility can feel crushing. Inspiring because you have the opportunity to shape not just your children's lives, but your grandchildren's lives and your great-grandchildren's lives. The legacy you're building will echo through generations.

Years from now, when your children are grown and raising their own families, they'll remember. They may not remember every word you said or every lesson you taught. But they'll remember how you made them feel. They'll remember whether you were present. They'll remember if you loved them well. They'll remember if your faith was real. And they'll pass those memories — those patterns, those values, those truths — on to their own children.

This is your legacy. Not your career accomplishments or your financial success or your achievements. Your legacy is the faith you've modeled, the love you've demonstrated, the character you've built, and the children you've raised to know and follow Jesus.

A Final Word

As you close this book and continue your journey, I want to leave you with this encouragement: You are not alone. The same God who called you to fatherhood is the same God who will equip you for it. The same God who commanded Joshua to be strong and courageous is the same God who walks with you today. The same God who gave Paul strength for every challenge is the same God who will strengthen you. The same God who is described as the perfect Father in heaven is the same God who will teach you how to father your children on earth.

He sees you. He knows the weight you carry. He understands the fears you face. He's aware of the challenges you're navigating. And He's with you. Every single day. In every moment. Through every season.

So keep going. Keep growing. Keep loving. Keep leading. Keep trusting. Keep showing up. Your faithfulness matters more than you can see. Your presence matters more than you know. Your love matters more than you can measure.

You're not just raising children. You're raising the next generation of world-changers, kingdom-builders, and difference-makers. You're not just going through the motions of daily life. You're building something eternal. You're creating a legacy that will outlive you.

And that, my friend, is worth every sacrifice, every struggle, every sleepless night, every moment of doubt, and every ounce of effort you pour into it.

So stand strong. Father strong. Love strong. Lead strong.

Your family needs you. Your children are counting on you. And God is with you.

The journey continues. And you're ready for it.

"Finally, be strong in the Lord and in his mighty power." — Ephesians 6:10

Now go. Be the father God has called you to be. Your family is waiting.

About the Author

Bruce Stapleton brings together corporate leadership, entrepreneurial success, and deep spiritual commitment in his work on Biblical fatherhood. This devotional draws from his primary text, *Fathering Strong - God's Blueprint for Leading Your Family*. His expertise stems from over 25 years of creating and teaching Christian adult education and over 10 years working with Urban Light Ministries' fatherhood initiatives, where he's worked alongside founder and President Pastor Eli Williams. Through this experience, Bruce has developed profound insight into the challenges modern fathers face and the Biblical solutions that can transform their families.

His innovative support for fathers shines through in the co-development of the "Fathering Strong" app, delivering daily inspiration and practical, Bible-based advice. Through his leadership of the Fathering Strong podcast and management of Urban Light Ministries' digital presence, Bruce has become a trusted voice in faith-based fatherhood education.

Bruce's corporate experience includes executive positions at NCR Corporation, where he led worldwide services marketing and strategic planning. His entrepreneurial spirit led him to create the award-winning Lifegevity program in preventive health and wellness. As a current college digital marketing instructor with both a Bachelor's in Business and Economics and an MBA, he brings both academic knowledge and real-world experience to his fatherhood teachings.

Bruce's perspective is uniquely shaped by his role as a father of four and grandfather of four, along with his 42-year marriage and active church ministry involvement. Readers find in his work an exceptional blend of practical experience, professional expertise, and spiritual wisdom, offering fathers a clear path to building stronger, faith-centered families.

For more resources go to:
www.fatheringstrongbook.com

Primary Text: Fathering Strong: God's Blueprint for Leading Your Family
Journal: Fathering Strong: Fatherhood Awakening and 30-day Devotional
and Journal
Fathering Strong Fatherhood Workshop - Participant Workbook
Fathering Strong Fatherhood Workshop - Facilitator Guide

Purchase at fatheringstrongbook.com.

Workshop for Churches
Interested in a fatherhood workshop? Contact
information@fatheringstrongbook.com for bundle discounts on
Fathering Strong resources.

Join a fatherhood community where you can connect with other
fathers, get support and encouragement throughout your
fatherhood journey, and become empowered to be the best dad
you can be. Join this free community today!

Join at www.fatheringstrong.com